Reason and Realpolitik

Books by Louis René Beres

The Management of World Power: A Theoretical Analysis (1973)

Reordering the Planet: Constructing Alternative World Futures with Harry R. Targ (1974)

Transforming World Politics: The National Roots of World Peace (1975)

Planning Alternative World Futures: Values, Methods and Models with Harry R. Targ (1975)

Terrorism and Global Security: The Nuclear Threat (1979)

Apocalypse: Nuclear Catastrophe in World Politics (1980)

People, States and World Order (1981)

Mimicking Sisyphus: America's Countervailing Nuclear Strategy (1983)

Reason and Realpolitik

U.S. Foreign Policy and World Order

Louis René Beres
Purdue University

LexingtonBooks
D.C. Heath and Company
Lexington, Massachusetts
Toronto

Library of Congress Cataloging in Publication Data

Beres, Louis René.
Reason and Realpolitik.

Includes index.
1. United States—Foreign relations—1945. 2. Atomic warfare. 3. Deterrence (Strategy). 4. United States—Military policy. 5. Civil rights (International law). I. Title
JX1395.B454 1984 327.73 83-49102
ISBN 0-669-07756-9 casebound
ISBN 0-669-07758-5 paperback

Published simultaneously in Canada

Printed in the United States of America

Casebound International Standard Book Number: 0-669-07756-9

Paperback International Standard Book Number: 0-669-07758-5

Library of Congress Catalog Card Number: 83-49102

For all who would choose to disobey

Contents

Figures and Tables

Figures

Table

Acknowledgments

This book owes a great deal to the remarkable people at Lexington Books. I am especially grateful to my editor, Jaime Welch, whose skill and sustained enthusiasm for the project make working with her a special pleasure; and to Pamela J. Walch, marketing manager, whose initial interest in the book made possible this second happy alliance between author and publisher. I also wish to thank Martha Hawkins for her demonstrated efficiency as editorial assistant and Marsha M. Forrest for her most capable and conscientious handling of the manuscript as production editor. Finally, my appreciation is offered to Cynthia Insolio Benn, who as copy editor has once again made her presence felt in a very sensitive and productive manner.

1 From Conflict to Cosmopolis: The World Order Imperative

During the last year of his tenure as Secretary of State, Henry Kissinger remarked to the Council of Ministers of the Central Treaty Organization: "The fundamental principles of U.S. foreign policy have been constant for the past 30 years, through all administrations—and they will remain constant. The American people have learned the lessons of history."[1] This statement is markedly self-contradictory, for if the American people have indeed learned the "lessons of history," they would surely prevail upon their leaders to *undo* the constancy of American foreign policy.

These lessons, if they teach us anything at all, point up the futility of America's strategy of realpolitik, a strategy founded upon the very principles that have ensured the oblivion of other great states. To suggest otherwise is to ignore the fact that policies of power politics have never succeeded in producing either justice or security. Unless these policies are now rapidly and completely transformed, they will produce the most intolerable conditions the United States and the world have ever known.

To transform these policies in a manner that reflects genuine learning from lessons of the past, we must first recognize the false premises that continue to shape our search for a durable and just peace in world affairs. Differences in rhetoric and style notwithstanding, these premises, articulated by Henry Kissinger in 1976, are still at the core of U.S. foreign policy:

> Peace rests fundamentally on an equilibrium of strength. The United States will stand by its friends. It accepts no spheres of influence. It will not yield to pressure. It will continue to be a reliable partner to those who defend their freedom against foreign intervention or intimidation.[2]

untrue

Each of these premises is entirely untrue:

> There is absolutely no logical argument or historical evidence to support the contention that a "balance of power" produces peace.[3]

> The United States will certainly not "stand by its friends" if such support is apt to produce devastating military consequences, a distinct possibility in today's apocalyptic age.

> The United States has always accepted the idea of "spheres of influence" and cannot afford to reject this idea within the existing structure of world power.
>
> The United States will necessarily yield to pressure if the probable benefits of this course are judged to exceed the probable costs. To suggest otherwise would be to suggest irrational national leadership in the U.S. foreign policy establishment.
>
> The United States will prove a "reliable partner" in defense of "freedom" only where such action is deemed consistent with the realpolitiker's assessment of national interest.

The United States, therefore, must begin to fashion its foreign policy behavior on a new set of premises, one consonant with the constraints of planetary conditions and the exigencies of national survival. Underlying these principles must be the understanding that this nation coexists with others on this endangered planet in a perilously fragile network of relationships. Racked by insecurities, poverty, and inequality, this network can no longer abide the conflictual dynamics that have shaped international relations since the sixteenth and seventeenth centuries.

Unless the United States, while it is still a preeminent (if not ascendant) power in the world, begins to understand that its own national interest must be defined from the standpoint of what is best for the world system as a whole, that interest will not be sustained. Instead, it will crumble along with the rest of a foreign policy edifice that is oblivious to its own self-destructive tendencies. Consider the following:

The nuclear arms race cannot last forever. In a world already shaped by some 6,000 years of organized warfare, it is hard to imagine that nuclear weapons will remain dormant amidst steadily accelerating preparations for nuclear war. Rather, the apocalyptic possibilities now latent in these weapons are almost certain to be exploited, either by design or by accident, by misinformation or by miscalculation, by lapse from rational decision or by unauthorized decision.

Since the dawn of the Atomic Age, the search for security through destructive weaponry has led only to increased insecurity. Although the world's stockpile of nuclear weapons now represents an explosive force more than 5,000 times greater than all the munitions used in World War II, the expansion of superpower arsenals continues at a frantic pace. And in the United States this expansion is undertaken from a policy perspective that ties successful deterrence to a capacity to "fight" a nuclear war that might be "protracted."

The situation is further undermined by the ever-hardening dualism of U.S.-USSR relations and by the associated American tendency to cast all such relations in zero-sum terms. Although the period from the Cuban missile crisis (1962) to the present was marked by a conscious commitment to avoid direct confrontations with the Soviet Union, there now seems to have developed an increased U.S. willingness to accept such confrontations as an essential requirement of rational competition in a decentralized world system. Moreover, wars have been increasing in frequency since 1945, from an average of nine a year in the 1950s to fourteen a year so far in the 1980s, a development that contributes to the likelihood of a direct conflict between the superpowers.[5]

There are also very serious problems with current U.S. foreign policy on human rights. Apart from this policy's disregard for moral and legal obligations, it is also contrary to our national interests. While this policy is cast in pragmatic terms, it should be apparent from the persistent failure of antecedent U.S. policies that it can never succeed.

In making anti-Sovietism the centerpiece of its policy on human rights, the United States has accepted an orientation to global affairs that is inherently self-defeating. During the next several years, the victims of U.S.-supported repression throughout the world will begin to overthrow their oppressors, creating successor governments with unquestionably anti-American leanings. In the fashion of Vietnam, Cuba, Nicaragua, and Iran, these governments will join the ever-expanding legion of states opposed to the United States. Sadly, this development will have been avoidable if only this country had remained true to its doctrinal foundations, opposing not only "leftist thugs" (President Reagan's characterization of the regime overthrown in Grenada) but all tyrannical regimes (that is, rightist thugs as well).

There has been no learning from lessons of the past. Although it is now perfectly clear that the Vietnam War might have been avoided if the United States had only understood the forces of revolutionary nationalism in the Third World, there is still no attempt to understand these forces. While it is now quite likely that early support for a still pro-American Ho Chi Minh rather than for his colonial masters might have created an ally instead of an adversary, the United States continues to advance its visceral counterrevolutionary ethos. What can this country hope to accomplish by standing alongside such pariah states as Chile and South Africa while unleashing forces to "destabilize" less repressive regimes? Whatever their deficiencies, these "totalitarian" regimes are spotless models of Jeffersonian democracy in contrast to the governments of our most "authoritarian" allies.

In considering these problems of United States foreign policy on nuclear strategy and human rights, we must also understand that they are interrelated. In one of the dominant ironies of the current situation, the presumed U.S. imperative to ignore human rights in anti-Soviet states as a requirement of national security makes nuclear war more likely. By its policy to align itself with right-wing juntas and other reactionary regimes, the United States enlarges the prospects for confrontation with the Soviet Union, either directly or by escalating involvement with surrogate forces. In Central America, for example, U.S. policies portend a transnational civil war, with authoritarian regimes and counterrevolutionary guerrillas backed by the United States fighting against leftist insurgents and revolutionary regimes backed by the Soviet Union.

With an understanding of these problems, this book points the way from America's realpolitik orientation to foreign policy making toward a new definition of national interest. The United States must now do away with its long-standing adherence to an ethic of social Darwinism in world affairs. To accept this imperative would be to indicate genuine learning from lessons of the past. To do otherwise would be to capitulate to a developing planetary predicament with literally catastrophic qualities.

What is this developing planetary predicament? In the most general terms, it is a condition of widespread insecurity, poverty, alienation, injustice, ecological spoilation, and economic inequality. More specifically,

The global arms race continues at a very fast pace while the security of nations continues to erode.

The governments of the developing nations spend as much on military programs as on education and health care combined.

The United States and the Soviet Union, although still pre-eminent in terms of the instruments of violence, are steadily losing real *power.* They also lag behind many other nations in terms of principal indicators of social well-being.

The use of torture and other forms of repression by governments against selected segments of their populations continues to grow.

The rich states are getting richer while the poor states are getting poorer.

The global environment is being depleted and poisoned all the time.

The normative expectations of international law remain widely unsupported by the foreign policy conduct of virtually all major states.

This is only the tip of the iceberg. Should we begin to penetrate the anesthetized universe of international relations scholarship, we would discover an almost measureless degree of human pain and despair, a configuration of suffering that demands an indictment of the entire system of world political processes. Such an indictment is an essential precondition for creative planetary renewal.

How might such renewal actually be accomplished? To answer this question, we must first try to answer the following antecedent question:

What should be the future goal of American foreign policy?

Our goal must be nothing less than the erection of a new pattern of thinking that defines national interests in terms of strategies that secure and sustain the entire system of states. By supplanting competitive self-seeking with cooperative self-seeking, the United States can move forward to the kind of global renaissance that is so desperately needed. By building upon the understanding that it is in America's best interest to develop its foreign policy from a systemic vantage point, our national leaders can begin to match the awesome agenda of world order reform with viable strategies of response. We require, in the final analysis, a policy that is based on the reaffirmation of humane purposes and the creation of a respected framework of international cooperation.

Such a policy has never been tried. With its membership in the United Nations, the United States has done little to move beyond the Westphalian dynamics of competition and conflict. Although it is certainly true that the UN Charter goes much further than the League of Nations Covenant in formalizing the replacement of self-help with the centralized determination and application of sanctions, this change has had no meaningful effect on the calculations and preference-maximizing behavior of states. For all intents and purposes, law continues to follow power in the United Nations and the organization itself remains an institutional reflection of the prevailing pattern of influence. The state of nations is still the state of nature.

Even so, much can be done to improve upon this condition. For the United States as well as for the rest of the world, survival requires a renunciation of the "everyone for himself" principle. It is no longer possible to describe as "realistic" a foreign policy that is at cross-purposes with the spirit of systemic well-being. The impersonal logic of possessive individualism is at odds with the imperatives of national and international life.

To illustrate the argument for transforming competitive inclinations to foreign policy into cooperative ones, consider the following analogy: The nations in world politics coexist in the fashion of herdsmen who share a common pasture and who feel it advantageous to increase the size of their respective herds. Although these herdsmen have calculated that it is in their own best interests to augment their herds, they have calculated incorrectly. This is the case because they have failed to consider the *cumulative effect* of their calculations, which happens to be an overgrazed commons and economic ruin.

In the manner of herdsmen in this analogy, American foreign policy elites continue to act as if the security of the state is coincident with national military power. Like the herdsmen, these elites fail to understand the cumultive effects of such reasoning, leading the nation and the rest of the world away from the intended condition of peace and security. Blithely unaware that its outmoded strategy of realpolitik is strikingly unrealistic, the American search for an improved power position inevitably generates a pattern of antagonisms that hinders rather than helps the search for an improved world order.

Consider still one more analogy. The nations in world politics are prone to act in the manner of an audience in a crowded movie theater after someone has yelled "Fire!" Confronted with a sudden emergency, each member of the audience calculates that the surest path to safety is a mad dash to the nearest exit. The cumulative effect of such calculations, however, is apt to be far worse than if the members of the audience had relied on some sort of cooperative plan for safety.

In the fashion of the movie audience, the United States continues to misunderstand that its only safe course is one in which its own well-being and security are determined from the standpoint of what is believed best for the world system as a whole. The path to security that is founded upon the presumed benefits of preeminence is destined to fail. If we want peace, then we must prepare for peace, not for war.

How might such preparations be accomplished? Most importantly, the United States must cease its tendency to identify national security with conditions that undermine the entire system of states. This tendency is itself derived from an underlying and overwhelming egoism, a national incapacity to imagine the total annihilation of the United States. E.M. Cioran, who speaks in the tradition of Kierkegaard, Nietzsche, and Wittgenstein, said, "Nature has been generous to none but those she has dispensed from thinking about death." In this he is only partly correct. Although it is true, as Freud noted, that "It is indeed impossible to imagine our own death,"[6] it is an effort that must be attempted. While some repression of the fear of death may be essential to happiness and well-being, it can—where it is too "successful"—make extinction more imminent. Similarly, states can impair their prospects for survival by insulating themselves from reasonable fears of collective disintegration.

American leaders must take heed. There are more things in heaven and earth than are dreamt of in their philosophy.

But what, exactly, are these "things"? What can actually be done to bring about the desired condition? How can the United States reroute its narrowly self-interested mode of foreign policy activity to a more promising global orientation? How can American leaders begin to build upon the understanding that it is in this country's own best interests to develop strategies of international interaction from a systemic vantage point?

Heraclitus tells us that: "Men who love wisdom must enquire into very many things" (Fragment 49). Following this advice, the United States must begin to inquire into the ways in which a more secure and just system of world order might be obtained. Ultimately, this inquiry must direct our national leaders to an appropriate reversal of current policy directions on the major issues of world politics: the issues of nuclear strategy and human rights. It is the purpose of the following chapters to assist in this inquiry with the recommendation of specific and far-reaching proposals.

Should we fail in the obligation to sustain and dignify human life on this planet, it will be because of a failure to recognize *ourselves* as the proper locus of responsibility. The idea that humankind produces its own misfortunes has endured for millennia. Aeschylus, Homer, and Hesiod were convinced that humankind's disregard for wisdom accounts for its history as a continuous bath of blood. Such disregard, at the core of human wrongdoing, spawns a sea of ruin, fathomless and impassable. In such a sea, comments the King of Argos in *The Suppliant Maidens,* "Nowhere is there a haven from distress."

The Greek idea of fate does not imply the absence of human control over events but an inevitable penalty for failing to cultivate justice and peace. Understood in terms of the American responsibility for a more harmonious system of planetary political life, this idea suggests a willingness to seize the initiative for survival while there is still time. Vitalized by genuine knowledge rather than the desolate clairvoyance of realpolitik, the United States could then confront the dying world of apocalyptic militarism and repression with wisdom and hope.

Before we proceed to examine how this might take place, however, let us consider the idea and development of the system we seek to transform, the system of realpolitik. In this connection it is important to note that while the reasonableness of power politics as an operational necessity has enjoyed broad acceptance since ancient times, its celebration as a virtue unto itself is of relatively recent origin. Although it has long been observed that states must continually search for an improved power position as a practical matter, the glorification of the state *qua* force is a development of modern times. Known as *Machstaat,* this glorification—representing a break from the traditional political realism of Thucydides, Thrasymachus, and Machiavelli—was fully elaborated in Germany. From Fichte and Hegel, through Ranke and von Treitschke, the modern conceptualization of realpolitik transformed alleged facts of international statecraft into values and description into prescription. The consequences of this transformation lie at the center of our current global crisis.

To chart this transformation, we may begin with Thucydides. In the *Melian Dialogues,* he tells of the argument offered by the Athenians to the Melians during the Peloponnesian War:

> Then we on our side will use no fine phrases saying, for example, that we have a right to our empire because we defeated the Persians, or that we have come against you now because of the injuries you have done us—a great mass of words that nobody would believe. And we ask you on your side not to imagine that you will influence us by saying that you, though a colony of Sparta, have not joined Sparta in the war, or that you have never done us any harm. Instead, we recommend that you should try to get what it is possible for you to get, taking into consideration what we both really do think; since you know as well as we do that, when these matters are discussed by practical people, the standard of justice depends on the equality of power to compel and that in fact the strong do what they have the power to do and the weak accept what they have to accept.

Similarly, in Book I of *The Republic,* Plato has Thrasymachus explain to Socrates that "justice is nothing else than the interest of the stronger." And Machiavelli, underscoring the dilemma of practicing goodness in an evil world, places force at the very center of his political theory. Yet, in each of these cases, the centrality of power is instrumental. It is founded not upon a preference for struggle, but upon the presumption that there is no practical alternative.

Plato's own view of the state very clearly implies more than the sustained capacity to outdo adversaries. For him, the aim of the state can never be linked to the accumulation of power. Rather, in the ideal state, the philosopher-king, nurtured by a system that recognizes knowledge as virtue, would embody the rule of pure reason. Thucydides, of course, lamented the sway of realpolitik, and even Machiavelli was careful never to assume that might was more than a necessary tool, that it was in any way a source of right.

The transformation of realpolitik from a practical principle of action to an end in itself drew major strength from the formulation of the doctrine of sovereignty in the sixteenth and seventeenth centuries. Conceived as a principle of internal order, this doctrine underwent a curious metamorphosis wherein it became a rationale of international anarchy. Established by Bodin as a formal juristic concept in *De Republica* (1576), sovereignty came to be regarded as power absolute and above the law. "Sovereignty," says Bodin, "is the absolute and perpetual power within a state. . . . it is unrestricted power." Understood in terms of the relations *between* states, this doctrine encouraged the notion that states are beyond any form of legal regulation in their dealings with each other.

In fact, Bodin certainly did not intend such an interpretation of his thinking. Reflecting an ancient ideal most prominently associated with Plato and Aristotle, Bodin's theory subordinates even the sovereign to a law that is superior, a fundamental or higher law determined by reason and divine law. The publication of *Leviathan* by Thomas Hobbes in 1651, however, reflected changed ideas. Believing that people need for their security a "common power to keep them in awe," Hobbes advanced the idea of sovereignty as truly absolute and illimitable. But even for Hobbes, the power and authority of the sovereign are contingent on the provision of security for individual human beings, on the understanding that the sovereign will assure protection in exchange for his omnipotence.

Far more drastic was Hegel's later identification of the state as "the march of God in the world." Reflecting an inversion of Plato's and Aristotle's view of the *polis* as a moral community wherein human capacities for rational and moral action could best be cultivated, this identification produced the following argument in the *Philosophy of Right:*

> The state is the actuality of the ethical Idea. . . . The state is absolutely rational inasmuch as it is the actuality of the substantial will which it possesses in the particular self-consciousness once that consciousness has been raised to consciousness of its universality. This substantial unity is an absolute unmoved end in itself, in which freedom comes into its supreme right. On the other hand, this final end has supreme right against the individual, whose supreme duty is to be a member of the state.

With such an idea the Lockean notion of a social contract—the notion upon which the United States was founded—is fully disposed of, relegated to the ash heap of history. While the purpose of the state, for Locke, is to provide protection that is otherwise unavailable in the state of nature to individuals, the "preservation of their lives, liberties and estates," for Hegel the state assumes its own rationale. Holding its own will as preeminent, standing above any private interests, the state creates an expanding pretext for *raison d'état* that displaces all hope for personal development and dignity. It is the spirit of the state, *Volksgeist,* rather than of individuals, that is the presumed true creator of advanced civilization. And it is in war, rather than in peace, that a state is judged to demonstrate its true worth and potential.

The implications of this view have been grasped by Harold Laski:

> What the state ordains begins to possess for you a special moral sanction superior in authority to the claim of group or individual. You must surrender your personality before its demands. You must fuse your will into its own. It is, may we not without paradox say, right whether it be right or wrong. It is a lack of patriotism in a great war to venture criticism of it. It has the right, as in this sovereign view it has the power, to bind your will into its own. They who act as its organs of government and enforce its will can alone interpret its needs. They dictate; for the parts there is no function save silent acquiescence.[7]

The Hegelian view of the state also stands in stark contrast to that of St. Augustine. Although it was never intended as a work of political theory, the

City of God advances an image of the state as a profoundly sordid, wicked institution. In the famous words found in Book IV, Chapter IV of his treatise, "Justice being taken away, then, what are kingdoms but great robberies? For what are robberies themselves, but little kingdoms?" So as to remove any doubts about what he intends, Augustine relates the following brief tale:

> Indeed, that was an apt and true reply which was given to Alexander the Great by a pirate who had been seized. For when that king had asked the man what he meant by keeping hostile possession of the sea, he answered with bold pride, "What thou meanest by seizing the whole earth; but because I do it with a petty ship, I am called a robber, whilst thou who dost it with a great fleet art styled emperor.

By this reasoning, Augustine does not argue that the state must always be a faithful image of wickedness, but that such a condition is always attendant upon the absence of justice. It follows that the state can be redeemed from evil where it becomes subject to justice. In this notion, Augustine's position is reminiscent of Cicero, for whom justice is not only a proper purpose of the state, but a condition of its very existence.

The idea of the state as a sacred phenomenon, an idea of continuing ascendancy in our own day, was formalized by the growth of fascism in the twentieth century. Fascism takes as its motto "Everything for the state; nothing against the state; nothing outside the state." In the words of Mussolini, "For the fascist, all is comprised in the State, and nothing spiritual or human exists—much less has any value—outside the State. In this respect, fascism is a totalizing concept, and the Fascist State—the unification and synthesis of every value—interprets, develops and actualizes the whole life of the people."[8]

Important roots of such thinking may be found in the *Addresses to the German Nation* of Johann Gottlieb Fichte, whose violent racism and nationalism made him a direct precursor of Nazism, and the writings of Heinrich Treitschke. According to Treitschke:

> The State is the people legally united as an independent power. . . . The State is Power for this reason only, that it may maintain itself alongside of other equally independent powers. War and the administration of justice are the first tasks of even the rudest barbaric State. . . . The highest moral duty of the State is to safeguard its power. The individual must sacrifice himself for a higher community, of which he is a member; but the State is itself the highest in the external community of men, therefore the duty of self-elimination cannot affect it at all. The Christian duty of self-sacrifice for something higher has no existence whatever for the State, because there is nothing whatever beyond it in world history; consequently it cannot sacrifice itself for anything higher. If the State sees its downfall confronting it, we praise it if it falls sword in hand. Self-sacrifice for a foreign nation is not

> only not moral, but it contradicts the idea of self-preservation, which is the highest thing for the State. Thus, it follows from this, that we must distinguish between public and private morality. The order of rank of the various duties must necessarily be for the State, as it is power, quite other than for individual man. A whole series of these duties which are obligatory on the individual, are not to be thought of in any case for the State. . . . War is the only remedy for ailing nations. The moment the State calls "myself and my existence are now at stake!?" social self-seeking must fall back and every party hate be silent. The individual must forget his own ego and feel himself a member of the whole; he must recognize what a nothing his life is in comparison with the general welfare. In that very point lies the loftiness of war, that the insignificant individual disappears entirely before the great thought of the State.[9]

Sadly, it is not only in the fascist states that one now finds the idea of the state as sacred. The Soviet Union, rejecting the generous cosmopolitanism of the *Manifesto* ("Working men of all countries, unite!") acts precisely as do other executioner states in pursuit of perceived national interests. And the United States, conceived in the principles of the Enlightenment, seems intent upon sacrificing its ideals at the altar of lethal, purposeless competition.

Today the leaders of the United States are not content with despising the spirit of the Age of Reason, the spirit that gave birth to their country. They also find it necessary to execrate it as a source of impiety. As a result they have fostered a spirit of realpolitik that goes far beyond the bounds of an earlier ancient pattern of reluctant pragmatism. In this spirit the perceived interests of the United States *are* the ultimate value, even though their lack of congruence with worldwide interests renders them self-destructive. A stand-in for the deity, this nation is now taken as a Godhead of which everything is anticipated, a self-proclaimed overseer of an unrelated global society.

Before this situation can be changed, the United States must begin to act upon entirely different principles of international relations, principles that are based not on the misdirected ideas of geopolitical competition but upon the spirit of cooperation. To make this possible, our leaders will need to understand that realpolitik proves its own insubstantiality, that it is an unrealistic principle whose effects are accentuated by the steady sacralizing of the state.

To begin to act in its own interests as well as in the interests of the world as a whole (since they are inextricably intertwined), the United States should draw upon the wisdom of Hugo Grotius, the seventeenth century classical writer on international law. Accepting the existence of law outside and above the state, Grotius understood that purposeful international relations cannot be based on relations of pure force. Although coexisting without an all-powerful authority above them, states must learn to regard themselves as members of a true society, one warranted by the overriding imperatives of justice and natural law. These principles are of the highest utility, and the community of states can never be preserved in their absence.

In the *Leviathan,* Chapter 13, Hobbes offers his well-known description of interstate relations:

> Kings and persons of sovereign authority, because of their independency, are in continual jealousies, and in the state and posture of gladiators; their forts and garrisons, and guns upon the frontiers of their kingdoms, and continual spies upon their neighbors; which is a posture of war.

It need not follow from this description, however, that to improve upon its position in this dreadful condition of war (by which Hobbes does not necessarily mean actual fighting, but rather "the known disposition thereto. . ." or cold war), each state must act in disregard of the common interest. Although there exists no "common power" to harmonize relations between them, states can learn to understand that their safety and long-term interests are tied to compliance with certain norms of global cooperation. There is, moreover, nothing utopian about such an idea; rather, as Grotius understood, a cooperative legal system amid the conditions of juristic equality is not only imaginable, but essential: "That as soon as we recede from the Law, there is nothing that we can certainly call ours."

With this understanding, states are urged to act on the basis of binding obligations in their relations with each other *in their own interests.* The United States must not be paralyzed by uncertainty over the probable reciprocity of the other states, by the fear that its own compliance with the normative obligations concerning peace and human rights will not be paralleled by other members of the community of states. This is the case, as the following chapters will seek to make clear, because the benefits of cooperative action in this community are no longer contingent on the expectation of a broad pattern of compliance. Since the prospect of a catastrophic end within the extant dynamic of realpolitik is so very likely, U.S. action according to world order imperatives would meet the criteria of rational action whatever the expected responses of other major states.

We should not assume, however, that U.S. initiatives toward world order would most likely go unimitated. If we can assume that leaders of other major states are also aware of the urgency of planetary conditions, their rational response to U.S. initiatives might well be far-reaching acts of reciprocity. Should such acts begin to take place, a new and infinitely more hopeful pattern of interaction could supplant the lethal lure of primacy, a pattern that could serve U.S. interests and ideals simultaneously. Should such acts fail to materialize, the net effect of U.S. initiatives would still be gainful, since nothing could be more futile than continuing on the present collision course.

In the beginning, in that primal promiscuity wherein the swerve toward power politics occurred, the forerunners of modern states established a system of struggle and competition that can never succeed. Still captivated by this system, the Unites States allows the spirit of realpolitik to spread, further and further, like a gangrene upon the surface of the earth. Rejecting all standards of correct reasoning, this spirit cannot impose limits upon itself. It continues to be rife despite its rebuffs; it takes its long history of defeats for conquests; it has never "learned" anything.

The United States now has a last opportunity to confront the spirit of realpolitik as a long-misguided design for action and to witness the eclipse of this spirit with jubilation. In the absence of such a confrontation, the time will come when future civilizations, such as they might be, will examine the skeletal remains of the last prenuclear war epoch with a deserved sneer. Thrashing about in the paleontology of international relations, they will get the impression that the flesh of this epoch was fetid upon its advent, that in any meaningful sense it never existed at all, that it was a cosmetic disguise that masked nothing.

Notes

1. Speech at opening of CENTO meeting, May 26, 1976, London, p. 1.
2. Ibid., p. 3.
3. Although the balance of power appears to have offered two relatively peaceful periods in history, the ones beginning with the Peace of Westphalia and the Congress of Vienna, the hundred-year interval between the Napoleonic Wars and the First World War was actually a period of frequent wars in Europe. The fact that the balance of power has been disastrously ineffective in producing peace during our own century hardly warrants mention. Moreover, the current preoccupation with "balance" in nuclear forces between the superpowers is certainly misconceived, since balance has nothing to do with credible deterrence. Historically, of course, a balance-of-power system was ushered in with the Peace of Westphalia in 1648, and has been with us ever since. The basic dynamics of this system were reaffirmed at the Peace of Utrecht in 1713, the Congress of Vienna in 1815, and the two World War settlements. Strictly speaking, neither the League of Nations nor the United Nations can qualify as a system of collective security. Rather, both are examples of international organization functioning within a balance-of-power world. As for world government, even the case of Imperial Rome does not, strictly speaking, fulfill the appropriate criteria, since the extent of its jurisdiction was coextensive with only a portion of the entire world.
4. Long even before Pufendorf suggested that by treaties of alliance

"no addition is made to the obligation of the natural law," writers and thinkers on world politics had questioned the deterrent value of collective defense. The key element of such skepticism lay in what was believed to be the demonstrated unreliability of states to honor their alliance commitments once the inducement of expected benefits had been replaced by the expectation of injury or loss. Treaties, observed Sir Thomas More, will be flagrantly disregarded wherever compliance is judged contrary to national interest. The Utopians do not enter into alliances because of the apparent ease with which treaty terms may be violated: "A treaty can never be bound with chains so strong, but that a government can somehow evade it and thereby break both the treaty and its faith."

After the appearance of *Utopia,* skeptical utterances concerning alliance reliability continued to emerge from prominent sources. Sir Francis Bacon, Edmund Burke, Thomas Paine, Alexander Hamilton, and a great many others expressed serious reservations about the reliability of alliance commitments. (See, for example, Francis Bacon, "The Wisdom of the Ancients," in A. Spiers, ed., *Bacon's Essays and Wisdom of the Ancients* (Boston, 1884); Edmund Burke, "Three Letters to a Member of Parliament on the Proposals for Peace with the Regicide Directory of France," Letter I, in *The Works of the Right Honorable Edmund Burke,* 5th ed., 12 vols. (Boston, 1877), vol. 5.; Thomas Paine, "Prospects on the Rubicon," *The Writings of Thomas Paine,* Moncure Daniel Conway, ed. (New York and London, 1906), vol. 2; and Alexander Hamilton, *The Federalist,* no. 15.)

Taken together, their principal argument points to the futility of placing dependence on treaties that have no other sanction than the obligations of good faith. No matter how solemn the oaths that confirm treaties of alliance, formal compacts and commitments are of themselves insufficient to assure compliance. It must also be that the interests of the partners are in close conformity. Like individual human beings, states are tied to one another not by papers and seals but by resemblances and sympathies. From this standpoint, Frederick the Great was surely guilty of understatement when he postulated as a "known truth in politics" that "the most natural and consequently the best allies are those who have common interests." There is, as Bacon points out, one true and proper confirmation of faith: "Necessity, or the danger of the State, or the securing of advantage."

With the advent of the nuclear age came renewed doubts. Where it was assumed that national leaders express their decisions in terms of Locke's principle of the supremacy of rights—failing to respect alliance obligations whenever noncompliance is deemed the more gainful course of action—the new possibility of alliance assistance invoking nuclear retaliation has made the viability of collective defense more doubtful than ever. It follows that current U.S. policy on nuclear support for NATO raises more eyebrows than hopes.

5. These assessments are supported by recent empirical work in the field. For example, in his very refined deductive theory about war, Bruce Bueno de Mesquita offers data that suggest a strong relationship between the level of risk that national leaders are willing to accept and the consequent likelihood of war. See his book *The War Trap* (New Haven, Conn.: Yale University Press, 1981).

6. See Freud's "Thoughts for the Times on War and Death," in James Strachey, ed., *The Complete Psychological Works of Sigmund Freud,* standard ed. (London, The Hogarth Press, 1953), vol. 14, p. 289.

7. See Harold Laski, *Studies in the Problem of Sovereignty* (New Haven, Conn.: Yale Uniyersity Press, 1917), p. 8.

8. Cited by John Herman Randall Jr., *The Making of the Modern Mind* (Cambridge, Mass.: Houghton Mifflin, 1954), p. 663.

9. See Heinrich Treitschke, *Selections from Politics,* Gowan, tr., pp. 24–25, cited by John Herman Randall, Jr., *The Making of the Modern Mind,* pp. 669–670.

2 U.S. Nuclear Strategy: Embracing Omnicide

In recent years the United States has moved toward a strategy that involves plans to fight and "prevail" in a nuclear war. Founded upon the grievous misunderstanding that fighting a nuclear war could represent a rational option, this strategy now represents the reductio ad absurdum of realpolitik thinking. Failing to recognize the difference between violence and power, it is a strategy that portends not only war, but oblivion.

At the same time the architects of current U.S. nuclear strategy must not be confused with earlier exponents of realpolitik. Although there is certainly a sharing of some basic assumptions about the proper course of statesmanship, traditional advocates of realpolitik have understood the essential difference between violence and power. Long before the Atomic Age, Machiavelli recognized the principle of an "economy of violence"[1] that distinguishes between creativity and destruction: "For it is the man who uses violence to spoil things, not the man who uses it to mend them, that is blameworthy."[2] Regarding war, Machiavelli counseled that victory need not be in the best interests of the prince, and that it might even produce an overall weakening of a state's position in world affairs.[3]

Even Clausewitz understood that war must always be conducted with a view to postwar benefit and that the principle of "utmost force" must be qualified by reference to the "political object" as the standard for determining the amount of force to be expended. In describing war as "a continuation of policy by other means," Clausewitz assumed that the object of war must always be a better peace. To resort to a war that can only produce desolation would clearly be senseless.

In a similar vein Nicholas Spykman, who served as the first director of the Yale Institute of International Studies before World War II, wrote: "In a world of international anarchy, foreign policy must aim above all at the improvement or at least the preservation of the relative power position of the state. Power is in the last instance the ability to wage *successful* war [emphasis added]."[5] This view, while falling short of a more enlightened world order perspective,[6] clearly distinguishes power from a resort to force that would destroy the vital interests of a state.

More recently, Hannah Arendt has elucidated a situation wherein the technical development of the implements of violence has now outstripped any rational justifications for their use in armed conflict. Hence, war is no longer the *ultima ratio* in world politics, the merciless final arbiter in international disputes but, rather, an apocalyptic chess game that bears no resemblance to earlier games of power and domination. In such a game if either "wins," both lose.[7]

Arendt's concern for the uncertainties of violence has roots in Tolstoy's, Schopenhauer's, and Joseph de Maistre's views about the chaos and uncontrollability of battles and wars,[8] and stands in marked opposition to the ranks of all passionate systematizers who deny the essential irregularity of battlefield activity. In the fashion of modern historians who seek "laws" to explain and predict the vagaries of human conduct on a global scale (Bossuet, Vico, Herder, Comte, Hegel, Buckle, Marx, Spengler, Toynbee, McNeill and others), U.S. strategists transform imperfect mosaics of military behavior into a structured "logic of events."[9] Entangled in metaphors and false assumptions, they display a singular failure to understand the truly human springs of action and feeling in world affairs.

More recently, Thomas Schelling has reminded us that since nuclear weapons make it possible to do monstrous damage to an adversary without first achieving victory, these weapons have reduced the importance of victory as an object of strategy. Consequently, nuclear weapons mark the beginning of a new epoch, one in which even the assurance of victory can offer no reasonable incentive to war. In this epoch rational leaders will look to their military forces not for victory, but for the bargaining influence that resides in latent force. And this influence will be degraded rather than enhanced by an announced willingness to fight a nuclear war to victory:

> Military strategy can no longer be thought of as it could for some countries in some eras, as the science of military victory. It is now equally, if not more, the art of coercion, of intimidation and deterrence. The instruments of war are more punitive than acquisitive. Military strategy, whether we like it or not, has become the diplomacy of violence.[10]

To counter the strategic mythmakers, students of world affairs would do well to reconsider Thucydides' account of the Peloponnesian War. Here, they would learn that the wellsprings of strategic behavior lie in the irrational and impulsive recesses of the human psyche. Here, they would encounter a memorable recitation of affairs in which the blind drives of honor and recklessness take precedence over considerations of safety and survival, a recitation that prefigures the consequences of excessive faith in rational models of nuclear warfare.

The conditions that arose in Classical Greece after the death of Pericles and the ascent of Cleon and Alcibiades in Athenian affairs have been repeated in countless episodes of human history. Understood in terms of the appraisals and prescriptions of the architects of U.S. nuclear strategy, these conditions point to an overweening pride and arrogance in counseling preparations for nuclear warfare, a pattern of hubris that underscores the urgency of Albert Einstein's warning at the beginning of the nuclear era: "The unleashed power of the atom has changed everything except our thinking. Thus, we are drifting toward a catastrophe beyond conception. We shall require a substantially new manner of thinking if mankind is to survive."[11]

Before we can achieve this new manner of thinking, we must learn to recognize that U.S. nuclear strategy is the antithesis of genuine thought. Assuming that because nuclear deterrence has worked thus far it will work forever, this strategy avoids any productive attempts at long-term security. In this respect it is reminiscent of the position of the chain smoker who contends that he has been smoking cigarettes for twenty-five years without ill effects and that smoking must therefore be safe. The real question, of course, is whether smoking will *ultimately* kill him. If it does, the final assessment of costs and benefits will turn out to be far less optimistic.

Just as significantly, the notion of deterrence embraced by the United States is not the notion that has been with us from the start. Today it is assumed that successful deterrence requires the perceived capacity to fight a nuclear war. Yet to meet its deterrence objectives, this country needs only to ensure that its strategic forces are sufficiently invulnerable and capable of penetrating to assuredly destroy the Soviet Union after riding out a first-strike attack. The United States does not need to take steps, as it currently is taking, to threaten the other side's retaliatory forces.

Another overwhelming deficiency of current U.S. nuclear strategy lies in its curious commitment to "balance" in U.S.–USSR nuclear forces. Although there is something that seems intrinsically attractive about such balance, there is no logical or historical argument to support this idea. As the French have long recognized, the capacity to deter is unrelated to equivalence.

As long as we can convince a rational Soviet adversary of our ability and willingness to destroy them after suffering a first strike, they will—whatever the existing balance of forces—be deterred. Even if we were to dispense with our entire intercontinental ballistic missile (ICBM) and Strategic Air Command (SAC) bomber forces, our submarine-launched ballistic missiles, (SLBMs), so long as they remain invulnerable, could ensure unacceptable levels of destruction. It is also true that a vastly superior U.S. nuclear arsenal could undermine deterrence if it signaled to the Soviets a plan for a U.S. first strike. Indeed, this is precisely the problem today, since the newest U.S. missiles are unsuitable for anything but an initial move to war.

It is wrong to assume, as does current U.S. nuclear policy, that neither side will ever strike first if it believes that by doing so it will bring down overwhelming carnage upon itself. Even perfectly rational states can be expected to preempt, whatever the expected consequences, if they believe that the other side is about to strike first. This is the case because in the theater-of-the-absurd logic of nuclear strategy, the country that strikes first in such a situation may expect to suffer less than if it waits to strike second. Sadly, almost everything now being done by the United States contributes to the Soviet fear of an American first strike.

The government of the United States has yet to admit to us, its citizens, that we are utterly defenseless against the effects of nuclear weapons. Reliable ballistic missile defense has never existed, nor will it ever exist. Ironically, the attempt to institute such defenses will be extraordinarily provocative, since it will encourage the Soviet Union to accelerate its offensive missile capabilities and even to preempt in the near term. The United States, for its part, lulled into complacence by the delusion of defense, might abandon remaining plans for arms control or even fulfill Soviet fears by preparing for an American first strike.

Our government has also not told us the truth about its plans to enlarge the American inventory of destabilizing nuclear weapons. During the next decade the United States will build about 17,000 new nuclear weapons. Spending on nuclear weapons is going up much faster than overall military spending. Under present plans the United States will spend $450 billion over the next six years preparing for nuclear war. And these monies will be used to create threatening counterforce systems that will engender a corresponding Soviet buildup and undermine nuclear deterrence.

Consider the MX. In spite of an initial rationale of improving survivability of this country's ICBM force, these prompt, hard-target-kill weapons will be placed in existing Minuteman silos. Their only real purpose, therefore, will be to fulfill distinctive counterforce mission objectives—that is, to destroy Soviet nuclear weapons and control systems during a nuclear war.

Nuclear warfighting, not survivability, is the only true purpose of MX. Indeed, the decision to deploy the new missiles in existing silos will degrade deterrence by occasioning a U.S. shift to "launch-on-warning" strategies—steps to fire these weapons upon confirmed attack rather than upon actual absorption of attack. With the adoption of such strategies, this country's major nuclear forces, because of the "use them or lose them" calculation, might be launched before Soviet weapons actually struck. It follows that a predictable result of MX deployment will be a greatly heightened probability of accidental nuclear war or even a Soviet first strike. If the Soviets were to respond to American moves with their own launch-on-warning measures (a response that could be instigated by the hard-target, countersilo qualities of the MX as well as by the U.S. acceptance of launch on warning), this country's MX deployment might even heighten the probability of a U.S. first strike.

Consider also the vaporous logic of Euromissiles. Amid the din and controversy surrounding the cruise and Pershing II deployments, our government has always overlooked the most vital point: these missiles could never actually be used in retaliation by a rational president of the United States. In the event of a Soviet/Warsaw Pact conventional attack against Western Europe, the scenario that gives rise to the NATO Euromissile deployments, a reprisal by any number of the projected 572 missiles directed against the Soviet homeland would lead to all-out nuclear war. Consequently, the threat to use these missiles to deter such an attack is wholly incredible. It could be argued in response that this threat might still be credible if the Soviets believed the U.S. president to be irrational, but if this were indeed the case, that country would have an irresistible and continuing incentive to strike first.

What if the Soviets should launch their nuclear weapons as a first offensive move of war? In such a case the cruise and Pershing II missiles would also prove useless because they would add nothing to our existing strategic capabilities. Whatever feeble damage-limitation benefits might accrue to the United States from its arsenal of counterforce-targeted nuclear weapons, they would not be improved by the firing of up to 572 new medium-range missiles. This is the case because there would be very little of the United States left to protect after the first round of Soviet attacks had been absorbed. Moreover, the United States does not even target Soviet submarine-launched ballistic missiles.

Why, then, did we deploy the new weapons? From the Soviet point of view, the only rational explanation must seem to lie in U.S. plans for a preemptive attack against their nuclear forces. Although the new missiles would, by themselves, do nothing to enhance the prospects for such an attack, it is conceivable that they would be judged useful to preemption in conjunction with existing Triad forces (ICBMs, SLBMs, and bombers). This judgment would follow from the Pershing IIs potential to strike such protected targets as command bunkers and nuclear storage sites in the Western USSR less than ten minutes after launch. And this entire first-strike appraisal must be considered together with parallel U.S. plans for the MX, antisatellite (ASAT) weapons, Ballistic Missile Defense (BMD), and improved civil defense.

We see, therefore, that since the Euromissile deployment is entirely useless as a deterrent, it suggests U.S. first-strike intentions to the Soviets. Such intentions are almost certainly not the purpose of these new weapons. All that matters, however, are Soviet perceptions. To alter these perceptions, we will have to convince the Soviets that NATO nuclear policy is animated not by aggressive designs but, rather, by certain overriding political considerations. Although this is probably the truth, it is hardly the argument one could expect this country to offer. Even if it were offered, its acceptance by an understandably suspicious adversary would surely be problematic.

Why is U.S. nuclear strategy so sorely misconceived? One important reason lies in the argument that the Soviets have been undergoing a far-reaching modernization and expansion of their own nuclear forces, and that we must be prepared to match these efforts. As one reads repeatedly in the newspapers, "They started it"! In fact, however, there is no reason to believe that mimicry is necessarily the correct strategy for the United States. Even if our worst-case assumptions about Soviet intentions are correct, it is not true that our interests are best served by escalating the levels of tension and uncertainty.

Where are the grown-ups? In developing a sensible nuclear strategy, the United States should be guided only by a meticulous comparison of the costs and benefits of alternative courses of action. Instead of commitments to the vague need for "matching" Soviet moves, our leaders must focus on the fact that there is no defensive use for any of the new American weapons. They must then come to understand the futility and danger of current American policy.

To do this, they must also take steps to overcome an underlying egoism referred to earlier, a basic incapacity to recognize the mortality of the United States. Looking backward, they must be sobered by the awareness of human history as an unending sequence of rise and fall. Assyria, Babylon, Egypt, Greece, Carthage, Rome, the Empires of Charlemagne and the Turks—all have been burned into the oblivion of the past. If we are to avoid a similar fate, we must first begin to experience some widespread shocks of recognition about our current nuclear collision course. Otherwise there is little hope that we—and perhaps all of humankind—can escape the last paroxysms of a shattered planet.

The realpolitik pretense that irreversible nuclear disaster cannot befall the United States represents a potentially fatal flight from reality. Our only hope for survival lies in facing squarely the possibilities of an apocalyptic nuclear winter. At the same time, to transform our primal terrors into constructive attempts at prevention, we must respond to the knowledge of our collective fragility not with paralysis, but with an informed rejection of officially sanctioned strategic myth—a myth that seeks to afford us a vision of reality that transcends both the world of science and common sense.

But what are the underlying bases of our current nuclear strategy? What accounts for the strategic mythmakers and their steady tilt toward *thanatos?* How can it be that the United States, now thoroughly dominated by what Lewis Mumford calls the military "megamachine," is so oblivious to its increasingly limited chances for survival? How is it that at a time when humankind can almost surely be counted upon to ensure the triumph of oblivion (the prototype of all injustice), the strategic mythmakers are so incapable of understanding what is happening?

What accounts for this curious asymmetry between reason and realpolitik? How can it be that our leaders continue to utter groundless conjectures with the seriousness of incantations? As captives of an archaic cosmology, do they seek to return to earlier systems of prelogical thought?

How can the United States remain so unaware of its own vulnerability? How, in view of our steady tilt toward nuclear war, can our leaders remain so tragically incapable of understanding what is taking place? How can they continue to advance an insipid nuclear theology amid the expanding popularization of medical and scientific critiques of strategic myth?

In the words of the author of *Ecclesiasticus,* "Vain hopes delude the senseless and dreams give wings to a fool's fancy" (34:1). How, then, can the administration continue to offer promises of normalcy in the post-nuclear war world? Do our leaders really believe that there will be a need for emergency change of address cards after the smoke has cleared? Do they really offer plans for the secure transport of sanitary napkins and credit cards to "relocation areas" without satirical intent?

In Book I of the *Odyssey,* Homer represents Zeus declaring to the Immortals: "What a lamentable thing it is that men should blame the gods and regard *us* the source of their troubles when it is their own wickedness that brings them sufferings worse than any which Destiny allots them." How, then, can the administration be so unmindful of its own responsibility for bringing us closer toward *thanatos?* Can they really believe that the prospects for a protracted peace are tied to the prospects for enduring a protracted nuclear war?

In *The Suppliants,* the play by Euripides, the Theban herald declares: "If death had been before their own eyes when they were giving their votes, Hellas would never have rushed to her doom in mad desire for battle." How, then, can the administration continue to assume we can "prevail" in a nuclear war with the Soviet Union? Do our leaders really fail to understand that current nuclear strategy concerns nothing less than the fundamental arrangements of human survival? In a world where stockpiled nuclear weapons can kill all life on earth in a way that would make impossible any further reproduction of living cells, do they fail to see that such weapons can destroy not only all of nature but even the natural relation of death to life?

Francis Bacon saw the medieval synthesis in philosophy as the work of profoundly cloistered men cut off from the roots of life. Because the schoolmen were immersed in closed systems of speculation rather than in observation, too little was done to "subdue and overcome the necessities and miseries of humanity.'' Today Bacon's insights, the insights of one who Alfred North Whitehead correctly called ''one of the great builders who constructed the mind of the modern world,'' apply equally well to the strategic mythmakers of the United States. Spinning ''laborious webs of learning'' without understanding and with ''small variety of reading,'' they narrow our intellectual horizons and substitute false certitude for necessary doubt. The result can only be an unheroic failure.

Bacon understood, in *The New Organon* and elsewhere, that ''idols and false notions'' can take possession of human understanding. To these he assigned names, calling the first class *Idols of the Tribe;* the second *Idols of the Cave;* the third, *Idols of the Market-place;* and the fourth, *Idols of the Theatre.*

The Idols of the Tribe ''have their foundation in human nature itself,'' and thus shed important behavioral light on the particular incoherence of current nuclear strategy.

The Idols of the Cave are the ''idols of the individual man,'' and flow from the unique characteristics and ''perturbations'' of each person. Drawing upon the Platonic myth of the cave, Bacon points out that ''every one has a cave or den of his own, which refracts and discolours the light of nature; owing either to his own proper and peculiar nature; or to his education and conversation with others; or to the reading of books, and the authority of those whom he esteems and admires; or to the differences of impressions.''

Understood in terms of current American nuclear strategy, the Idols of the Cave find expression in opportunism, thoughtlessness, and the false learning of strategic planning. They also find expression in other explanations of present policy, explanations to which we will soon turn.

The Idols of the Market-place are formed ''by the intercourse and association of men with each other.'' These false notions impair human understanding through the abuse of discourse wherein ''ill and unfit choice of words'' obstructs the search for genuine meaning. As the Idols that ''throw all into confusion and lead men away into numberless empty controversies and idle fancies,'' these notions find particular expression in the abstract speculations of strategic game theory.

Bacon's fourth and final class of Idols that ''beset men's minds'' is described as Idols of the Theatre. As false notions ''which have immigrated into men's minds from the various dogmas of philosophies, and also from wrong laws of demonstration,'' these Idols, representing ''worlds of their own creation after an unreal and scenic fashion,'' are manifest in the intellectual deficiencies of current American nuclear strategy, the closed universe of strategic gaming and the administration's identification with apocalyptic symbolization.

Let us look more closely at the particular manifestations of these idols in current nuclear policy. What are the specific answers to the question: "How can we explain the form and direction of current U.S. nuclear strategy?"

One answer is simply *opportunism.* The manufacture of strategic myth in the United States is a growth industry. Throughout the corridors of government and selected think tanks, Babbit caricatures turned scholars have discovered that there is both fame and fortune in the encouragement of facile nuclear machismo. It is a small matter that their recommendations are *wrong.* They sell!

In this connection military-industry firms in the United States enjoy a particularly sympathetic ear in the government. Faced with the need for sustaining lucrative contracts with the Department of Defense, these firms lobby the Pentagon, the Congress, and the White House in a fashion that produces a particular "need" for certain nuclear weapons systems. And with these weapons, of course, come strategies for their use. The entire system is strangely backward from the standpoint of defense, but it continues to operate with great success for the firms.

Such opportunism is especially difficult to combat during a period of high unemployment. At a time when anything that might threaten further joblessness is political anathema, the prospect of putting additional people out of work by cutting the military budget is clearly infeasible. This is not to suggest that military spending is good for the economy (it clearly is not), but that once a large military-dependent private sector already exists, it is—especially in periods of high unemployment—effectively immune from curtailment.

A second answer is *thoughtlessness.* By this I mean not the ordinary sense of the word, a lack of caring, but, rather, the meaning given by Hannah Arendt: the literal inability to think.

Wherever one turns today in the corridors of power, one encounters a marked incapacity to deal with a complex reality. Awash in gobbledygook, the administration seeks to make nonsense sensible. Instead, it is only making thinking impossible.

Why should this be so? One possible reason lies in the inherent attractiveness of simplicity to those who are unaccustomed to the stress of genuine thought. In this connection one is reminded of Ludwig Wittgenstein's statement from his work *On Certainty:* "Remember that one is sometimes convinced of the *correctness* of a view by its *simplicity* or *symmetry;* i.e., these are what induce one to go over to this point of view. One then simply says something like: *'That's how it must be.'*"

We may also turn to Plato for guidance. Plato's theory seeks to explain politics as an unstable realm of sense and matter, an arena formed and sustained by half-truths and distorted perceptions. In contrast to the stable realm of immaterial Forms, from which all genuine knowledge must be derived, the political realm is dominated by the uncertainties of the sensible world. Understood in terms of this country's misdirected nuclear strategy, Plato's wisdom suggests a condition wherein the hegemony of appearance over reality has reached its highest stage of development. With this strategy, the administration—already beholden to various idols—has sanctified the world of political inconscience.

Thought is synonymous with imagination, but the strategic mythmakers are prisoners of a subculture that can only use and reuse the same fixed categories of expression. Tantalized by falsehoods, the mythmakers offer a strategic void in place of correct inference. Having reached the point where life and death, reality and imagination, fact and fantasy have ceased to be seen as contradictory, their thought is turned inward upon itself, representing not critical analysis but primal ritual.

As we have already seen, nuclear weapons can serve the requirements of deterrence only where they threaten life and property. Since they are inappropriate tools for the military commander, the deployment of counterforce weapon systems is entirely misconceived. Whatever the rationale for such deployment, the United States now displays a marked incapacity for understanding the logic of nuclear deterrence, an incapacity that might be best explained by Bertrand Russell's observation in *Principles of Social Reconstruction* (1916): "Men fear thought more than they fear anything else on earth—more than ruin, more even than death."

A third answer to our question lies in the anesthetized nature of strategic thinking. By dealing only with abstractions of flesh and blood reality, the administration has lost sight of the concrete character of a nuclear war. To reverse this condition, it needs to confront the imagery of extinction with unaverted gaze and to understand that the fantasies of the infernal are part of our recent history.

Everything is possible! The chronicles of hell that offer insight into a world after nuclear war exist not only in art and literature, but in the genocidal reflexes of the twentieth century. It is from these visions of omnicide, as well as the portents of Dante and the panels of Bosch, that our country should draw its strategic understanding.

A fourth answer is psychopathology. However disturbing to consider, it is altogether possible that the advancement of falsehoods in the face of overwhelming evidence is, in certain cases, a function of mental illness. This sort of answer is fraught with difficulties, but it ought not to be dismissed out of hand.

Depending upon his degree of affliction, the schizophrenic is one who has more or less cut off relations with the world outside. Withdrawn into a private world, his social and intellectual judgments are routinely uninformed by the "facts" of his surroundings. With such an understanding, it is difficult to rule out schizophrenia as part of a possible explanation of strategic mythmaking.

In offering this explanation, I am aware, of course, that the definition of schizophrenia has varied greatly throughout the course of modern psychiatric history and that today's community of psychiatrists shares no greater unity of view about this syndrome than their forebears. The symptoms of this disorder are so diverse, its clinical complications so numerous, and its treatments so varied that conceptual utility is problematic at best. Certainly the classic descriptions of schizophrenia make this clear.

Yet, our present concerns do not call for clinical specificity. Even though one is cautioned to look for schizophrenia almost anywhere in the vast array of psychopathology, even behind the mildest and least dysfunctional of symptoms, our interest in this disorder lies not in systematic differentiation from related syndromes but in broad contrasts between psychopathic and "normal" behaviors. Unconcerned with the issues that interest psychiatric theorists and clinicians (e.g., statistical description, biochemical correlates and pharmacological treatment) we look only to the explanatory possibilities that lie latent in impaired mental functions. Whether or not schizophrenia is a disease like any other disease (having an etiology, pathogenesis, course, prognosis, and outcome), it defines a useful set of boundaries around human behavior for understanding the bases of strategic mythmaking.

With this in mind, let us consider the speculations of Erich Fromm. According to Fromm's work, *The Anatomy of Human Destructiveness,* schizophrenia is often linked to other types of psychotic processes. In this connection some of the strategic mythmakers may be true bureaucratic necrophiles—lovers of death whose sterile inclinations occasion them to salute nuclear war as liberation. Rejecting T.S. Eliot's advice that "It is no longer possible to find consolation in prophetic gloom," they urge us to prepare for omnicide as healer.

Such prescriptions are, without question, founded upon the spirit of atrophy and decay. This spirit must be distinguished from the usual clinical picture of necrophilia, wherein death is associated with corpses, but it is undeniable that the persons involved may still be attracted by the prospect of a world that is no more than the sum of lifeless artifacts. While the symbols of death have been transformed from objects of putrefaction to shiny engines of aluminum, steel, and glass, it is still the world of no-life that animates the spirit of today's strategic mythmakers. For them satisfaction may flow from the cult of antilife and aliveness may be the essence of anathema.

Yet there is nothing about these inclinations toward *thanatos* that suggests deliberate evil. In contrast to Freud's view, which is focused very specifically on base motives, the explanation of strategic necrophilia may be entirely consistent with good intentions. Indeed, in considering these circumstances, one is reminded of the statement by Albert Camus: "It seems to me that every one should think this over. For what strikes me, in the midst of polemics, threats and outbursts of violence, is the fundamental good will of every one."

It may even be that the strategic mythmakers are animated by an overriding wish to avoid evil and that their encouragement of policies that hasten nuclear war is the result of their commitment to all that is good in national and international affairs. As Ernest Becker points out in his *Escape from Evil:* "Men cause evil by wanting heroically to triumph over it, because man is a frightened animal who tries to triumph, an animal who will not admit his own insignificance, that he cannot perpetuate himself and his group forever, that no one is invulnerable to try to demonstrate it."

If we accept this view, that evil flows from the logic of the heroic, we must also accept that it is humankind's ingenuity rather than its animal nature that propels our journey to the outer limits of misfortune. Tortured by the knowledge of our own mortality and by the prospect of extinction with insignificance, we seek to transcend our unbearable fate through culturally standardized systems and symbols of heroism. Searching for a heroic victory over death by trafficking in pure power, man must inevitably create evil—not in pursuit of debased ideals, but for purity, goodness, and righteousness.

Following from all of this is a fifth explanation for the current conditions of strategic myth. This explanation, for lack of a better term, is human *ordinariness.* Understood in these terms, it is not mental illness, but normal human nature, that gives rise to strategic falsehoods.

Accepting the primacy of unfettered social Darwinism in world politics, the strategic mythmakers willingly place all human energies at the disposal of the military megamachine. Observing such behavior, we may convincingly dispose of the idea that only psychopaths could be responsible for such defective reasoning about nuclear weapons and national security. At the same time, by refusing to push our most profound deficiencies into the realm of mental illness, we invite ourselves to confront the most tragic aspect of current world politics—the banality of evil.

In *Orestes,* Euripides has Electra declare, "O human nature, what a grievous curse thou are in this world!" The capacity to commit terrible deeds lies latent in all human beings. And this capacity, in an ironic kind of complementarity, is bound up very closely with our all-encompassing (if not always conscious) fear of death. Much of human destructiveness may well have its roots in natural processes where we originally seek nothing more than to feel alive.

This idea is captured with particular insight by Eugene Ionesco in his "Diaries."

> I must kill my visible enemy, the one who is determined to take my life, to prevent him from killing me. Killing gives me a feeling of relief, because I

> am dimly aware that in killing him, I have killed death. My enemy's death cannot be held against me, it is no longer a source of anguish, if I killed him with the approval of society: that is the purpose of war. Killing is a way of relieving one's feelings, of warding off one's own death.

The human need for transcendence can be satisfied both by acts of creation and by acts of destruction. Human nature is neither innately good nor evil, but in a continuous flux between the two poles. Thus, says Erich Fromm in *On Disobedience,* "The ultimate choice for man, inasmuch as he is driven to transcend himself, is to create or to destroy, to love or to hate."

There is, then, a choice. But it is usually limited by the demands of the omnivorous State. The result of such limitation, wherein the state subordinates all moral sensibilities to the idea of unencumbered jurisdiction, was foreseen in the 1930s by José Ortega y Gasset. In *The Revolt of the Masses,* Ortega correctly identifies the state as "the greatest danger," mustering its immense and unassailable resources "to crush beneath it any creative minority which disturbs it—disturbs it in any order of things: in politics, in ideas, in industry." Set in motion by individuals whom it has already rendered anonymous, the state establishes its machinery *above* society so that humankind comes to live *for* the state.

This brings us to a sixth explanation for the contradictions of current nuclear strategy: the continuing infatuation with apocalyptic symbolization.

With its plans to "prevail" in a "protracted" nuclear war against an "evil empire," the administration's nuclear strategy now resembles a scheme for the final battle. Since all apocalyptic belief is a way of overcoming what Mircea Eliade calls the "terror of history," (*Cosmos and History: The Myth of the Eternal Return*), this strategy issues forth from a desperate need for order. Unwilling to be confused by an overwhelming array of facts, our leaders turn to the apocalypse as an alternate force of "understanding." Reason is crushed by such a force.

In this sense America's current nuclear strategy bears a strange affinity to certain ancient Hebrew writings that were found in caves near the Dead Sea. By its preparations for an apocalyptic war, it resembles the Qumran text called *The War of the Sons of Light and the Sons of Darkness.* While the Scrolls declare that God, with his human and celestial partisans, will do battle against the forces of Belial, the Prince of Darkness, the U.S. administration envisions a conflagration between secular superpowers that are the embodiment of good and evil.

The administration, of course, may not recognize such resemblance. The Brotherhood of Qumran, regarding itself as the true Congregation of Israel, *knew* that it was preparing for the ultimate contest. The president and his appointed officials, however, seem to believe that by preparing for nuclear war they might be able to prevent its occurrence. For the authors of the Scrolls, the task was to bring man back, in an age of apostasy, to the true way before the final judgment. For the government of the United States the task seems to be to avoid nuclear war by displaying an exaggerated willingness to fight such a war. If, however, nuclear war becomes inevitable, our leaders urge that we learn to recognize the benefits of rational war-waging, that we begin to value the Apocalypse. In this connection, we are reminded of Michel Foucault's idea in *Madness and Civilization:* "It is no longer the end of time and of the world which will show retrospectively that men were mad not to have been prepared for them; it is the tide of madness, its secret invasion, that shows that the world is near its final catastrophe; it is man's insanity that invokes and makes necessary the world's end."

In its picture of Last Things, Jewish tradition concerning the final conflict identifies the adversaries of God primarily with the unrighteous elements among man, the heathen who serve the Prince of Darkness. To prepare for this conflict, *The War of the Sons of Light and the Sons of Darkness* offers a precise plan, one that conforms to standard Roman patterns of military organization, procedure, and strategy. American plans for fighting a nuclear war are also specific. Described in portions of a 125-page document leaked to *The New York Times* in Spring 1982, this five-year military program for the United States envisions precise cycles of moves and countermoves that might take place over an extended period of time.

According to the Scrolls, salvation was to come only after victory in the struggle against the iniquitous Sons of Darkness. Although current American nuclear strategy has never consciously *sought* a nuclear Armageddon, several of its principal exponents have fantasized publicly about its near inevitability and even its long-term benefits. And while no administration spokesmen have suggested that a post-Apocalypse world order would be anything but catastrophic, they have suggested that "survival is possible."

Though attached to this world, such suggestions do not really belong to it: there is something nonterrestrial about their formulations. Reflecting a desolate "perspicacity" that eludes our perceptions, their invitation to finality is merely a memory projected into the future, a nostalgia for distant imaginations of redemption converted to public policy. But it is their fate, even as they aspire to happiness, to encourage only necropolis.

Nonetheless, like all forms of apocalyptic thinking, U.S. nuclear strategy holds out hope for the suffering righteous. Seeking to console believers with the hope of coming vindication, it tries to rouse them to resist and to prepare in order to endure. It is, of course, only a small matter that survival is not possible in a nuclear war. God is assuredly on our side.

Contrary to its own policy pronouncements, current American nuclear strategy does not flow from careful comparisons of the costs and benefits of alternative courses of action. Rather, its origins are embedded in traditional apocalyptic hopes for the future that involve the transcendence of death. And since all apocalyptic thinking is manifested in political rhetoric, these hopes are now tied to the state that is the very embodiment of Goodness: the United States.

Today, as Lewis Mumford observed in *The Myth of the Machine: The Pentagon of Power,* all human energies have been placed at the disposal of the state's military "megamachine" with whose advent we are all drawn unsparingly into a "dreadful ceremony" of worldwide human sacrifice. Causing evil by wanting to overcome it, the state accepts a formula whereby the killing of legions of outsiders would placate invisible powers of death by expiation. Rejecting the illusion of its own immortality, the state seeks to transcend its vulnerability through identification with ancient patterns of eschatological thinking.

Dostoevsky understood that killing is often distasteful, but that the distaste is swallowed if it is essential to true heroism. And what greater heroism can there be than to take up arms in the final battle against Evil. By characterizing the struggle with the Soviet Union in starkly ideological terms, the administration prods its people to accept omnicide with pure hearts. Encouraged by politics and protected by the glorious anonymity of the state, the tendency to omnicide will know no bounds. The ordinary citizen has been galvanized to become a part of a furious torrent of unparalleled destructiveness, a torrent that will consume him or her together with all others.

In a world in which the idea of the state has become a perfect stand-in for God, the United States now finds it easy to assert its own sacredness. Reflecting a combination of transcendence and proximity, it is, as Jacques Ellul has pointed out in *The New Demons,* "the ultimate value which gives everything its meaning. It is a providence of which everything is expected, a supreme power which pronounces truth and justice and has the power of life and death over its members. It is an arbiter which is neither arbitrary nor arbitrated, which declares the law, the supreme objective code on which the whole game of society depends." The fact that it is prepared to become an "executioner state" is not hard to reconcile with its commitment to Goodness, since both mass butchery and progress "are expressions of the sacred and are mutually related through the sacred."

With its current nuclear strategy, therefore, the United States reflects a peculiarly archaic view of the world, one wherein the earth exists preeminently as background, as location of the great drama God has prepared for humankind. In this view the earth is still the center of the universe, beyond which lie the incorruptible firmament and finally the Empyrean of the

Elect. Yet, as Anatole France reasoned in *The Garden of Epicurus,* we are done with the twelve heavens; the solid vault of the firmament is shattered. Beyond the planets we discover no longer an abode of the blessed but "a hundred million rolling suns, escorted by their cortege of obscure satellites invisible to us."

In the midst of this infinity of worlds, our own sun is but a bubble of gas; our earth a mere speck surrounded by unfathomable depths of silence. Understood in terms of current American nuclear strategy, this suggests the need for a new worldview, one in which an improved awareness of humankind's place in the universe can spawn a desacralization of the state and the end of apocalyptic thinking in world affairs. In abandoning the ruins of apocalyptic thought, the United States could begin to confront the ashes of endless ruins-in-the-making not as a victim, but as a gifted elegist. Before this can happen, however, our leaders must profit from the wisdom suggested by Nietzsche's preface to the polemic *On the Genealogy of Morals,* that we must cease to look for the origin of evil "*behind* the world."

What, then, is to be done? The answer is clear! We require nothing less than a new nuclear regime—a system of reciprocal obligations, force structures, and doctrinal postures, based upon an overriding commitment to nuclear war avoidance. Rather than add to the existing burden of corrosive stresses and contradictions between the superpowers, such a regime could create the conditions of cooperation, commonality, and pluralism. To prevent nuclear war between the superpowers, the United States must promptly replace overworked scenarios of nuclear gamesmanship with a new awareness of the long-term futility of arms racing.

In the final analysis the chances for a successful detachment from strategic arms racing will depend upon concrete steps taken to negotiate a viable agreement in the Strategic Arms Reduction Talks (START), an agreement on nuclear arms limitation in the European theater, a comprehensive nuclear test ban, a U.S. renunciation of the right to first use of nuclear weapons, a joint nuclear freeze, and ever-expanding nuclear-weapon-free zones. And these steps will depend upon a prior understanding by the superpowers that the primary arena of nuclear war avoidance is *intra*national. Understood in terms of reversing America's current nuclear strategy, this means that we require a rapid and far-reaching disengagement from existing patterns of counterforce targeting and from preparations for nuclear warfighting. It is only when such disengagement is complete that a viable arms control agenda can be implemented.

The ultimate objective of START must be an agreement wherein both sides undertake substantial reductions in strategic forces. Before this objective can be realized, there must take place a progressive transformation of conflictual foreign policies within the United States and the Soviet Union and an incremental development of arms control and nonproliferation strategies. With the appearance of such a regime, the START process could proceed to the negotiation of actual reductions in strategic forces, and meaningful disarmament negotiations could be extended to other states.

While it is urgent to get underway with real reductions in strategic forces, it would be a mistake to seek these reductions prematurely. An improved nuclear regime must be constructed bit by bit. Although it would be a serious error to abandon disarmament for less ambitious arms control remedies, it would be just as debilitating to seek disarmament before such remedies are in place. Before the superpowers can be expected to trust that disarmament measures will be generally enough respected, they will require antecedent assurances of reciprocal cooperation and goodwill.

The proposed American initiatives only *appear* risky. In actuality they are considerably less dangerous than continuing on the present course. Even if the United States were to experience certain difficulties in getting the Soviet Union to reciprocate these initiatives, there would be no deleterious effect on American security. Indeed, the net effect on American security of even unreciprocated initiatives would be gainful. This is the case, as we have seen already, because current U.S. nuclear policy is founded upon weapons systems and strategies that actually *undermine* the system of mutual deterrence. Contrary to the conventional wisdom that suggests American initiatives must lead to unilateral disarmament, the proposed initiatives would leave this country with a still-awesome and secure potential for nuclear retaliation. This is because the United States would seize these deescalatory initiatives without diminishing its assured destruction capacity vis-à-vis the Soviet Union.

Improving the survivability of the U.S. strategic triad must continue to be an overriding objective of this country's defense posture. But it is altogether clear that this objective can be satisfied without moving toward the capacity for expanded counterforce strikes, expanded theater nuclear force deployments, and expanded preparations for nuclear warfighting. Indeed, as Soviet countermoves must always be considered, a progressive American return to the relative safety of minimum deterrence represents the only prudent path to stability and survival.

To survive into the future, the United States must learn to recognize that its Soviet adversary has much to gain from a mutual and graduated process of deescalation and conflict reduction and that each side now has the national technical means to verify the other's compliance with this process. Moreover, even if it denies a Soviet willingness to enter into such a process, the United States must come to understand that the risks of unreciprocated initiatives toward minimum deterrence and denuclearization are very low in comparison to the risks of the expanded nuclear competition. As C.P. Snow, the English physicist and writer, once said: "On the one side, we have a finite risk. On the other side, we have a certainty of disaster. Between a wish and a certainty, a sane man does not hesitate."[12]

The capacity to prevent nuclear war is inseparable from a new consciousness by our national leaders. Amid the precarious cross-currents of implausible strategic myths, the United States and the Soviet Union must both undertake prodigious efforts to resist the lethal lure of primacy. Poised at the edge of history, the superpowers must infuse their foreign policies with a new understanding of partnership, with each other and with the entire family of nations. The Enlightenment philosopher, Jean Jacques Rousseau, once remarked: "The majority of nations, as well as of men, are tractable only in their youth; they become incorrigible as they grow old." Understood in terms of the superpower imperative to change direction in the search for peace, this suggests that unless these nations achieve such a change before losing their "youth" the chances for later success may be lost forever.

Notes

1. See the discussion of this principle in Sheldon S. Wolin, *Politics and Vision: Continuity and Innovation in Western Political Thought* (Boston: Little, Brown, 1960), pp. 195–238.
2. See *Discourses,* I, cited by Wolin, ibid., p. 221.
3. See *Discourses,* II, cited by Wolin, ibid., p. 222.
4. See *On War,* Book VIII, Chapter 6B, "War Is an Instrument of Policy" (Princeton, N.J.: Princeton University Press, 1976).
5. See Nicholas John Spykman, *America's Strategy in World Politics: The United States and the Balance of Power* (New York: Harcourt, Brace, 1942), p. 41.
6. For an elucidation of this perspective, see Louis René Beres, *People, States and World Order* (Itasca, Ill.: F.E. Peacock, 1981); Saul H. Mendlovitz, ed., *On the Creation of a Just World Order* (New York: The Free Press, 1975); and Richard A. Falk, *A Study of Future Worlds* (New York: The Free Press, 1975).
7. See Hannah Arendt, *On Violence* (New York: Harcourt, Brace and World, 1970), p. 3. A similar argument is advanced by Arthur Koestler in the Prologue to his *Janus: A Summing Up* (New York: Random House, 1978).
8. See the discussion of these thinkers by Isaiah Berlin, *The Hedgehog and the Fox* (New York: Simon and Schuster, 1957).

9. For an illuminating argument on the indeterminacy of history, see Jacques Barzun, *Clio and the Doctors: Psycho-History, Quanto-History, and History* (Chicago: The University of Chicago Press, 1974).

10. See Thomas C. Schelling, *Arms and Influence* (New Haven, Conn.: Yale University Press, 1966), p. 34.

11. See Albert Einstein, "Atomic War or Peace," *Atlantic Monthly,* November 1945.

12. See C.P. Snow, "Risk of Disaster or a Certainty," *The New York Times,* Op. Ed., August 17, 1981. C.P. Snow died in 1980. This article is excerpted from a speech, delivered in 1960, published in *The Physicists* (Boston: Little, Brown, 1981).

3 U.S. Nuclear Strategy: Enhanced Civil Defense

A core concept of current U.S. nuclear strategy is the plan for improved civil defense of the nation's population. In conformance with the developing countervailing strategy of deterrence, this country is now embarked upon a far-reaching campaign to sustain U.S. populations in the aftermath of Armageddon. Spawned by the provocative premises of realpolitik, this campaign is expected to inhibit Soviet adventurism by warning our adversary of our willingness to fight. The essence of this campaign is known as crisis relocation planning (CRP).

As an "enhanced" form of civil defense, such planning calls for the "temporary relocation" of approximately 150 million people from about 400 "high-risk" metropolitan and defense-related areas to approximately 2,000 allegedly safer "host" areas during periods when nuclear attack appears imminent. With such relocation, the Federal Emergency Management Agency (FEMA), the agency charged with crisis response, claims that we can double the number of Americans who could survive a nuclear war. Since FEMA estimates that about 40 percent of the population could survive such a war in the absence of relocation, this means that CRP is designed to bring the survival rate to 80 percent.[1] In short, U.S. policy suggests that with CRP measures in place, a nuclear war would be survivable for most Americans.[2]

Indicated on the FEMA map titled "High-Risk Areas" are (1) 52 so-called counterforce areas containing U.S. strategic offensive forces—9 ICBM complexes, about 40 SAC bases, and 3 ballistic missile submarine ports; (2) some 250 metropolitan areas of more than 50,000 population; and (3) about 100 additional areas with other important military and economic installations.[3] (See figure 3-1.) These risk areas cover only 2 to 3 percent of the land area of the United States but contain about two-thirds of our population and a somewhat higher percentage of our industry. Counterforce areas are also illustrated by the map, "Prime U.S. Military Targets" from the Center for Defense Information (figure 3-2).

FEMA believes that the population at risk can be protected by providing high-performance blast shelters in cities *or* by relocating (evacuating) the people to low-risk host areas outside the risk areas.[4] The agency's over-all plan for Nuclear Civil Protection (NCP) is founded upon the two

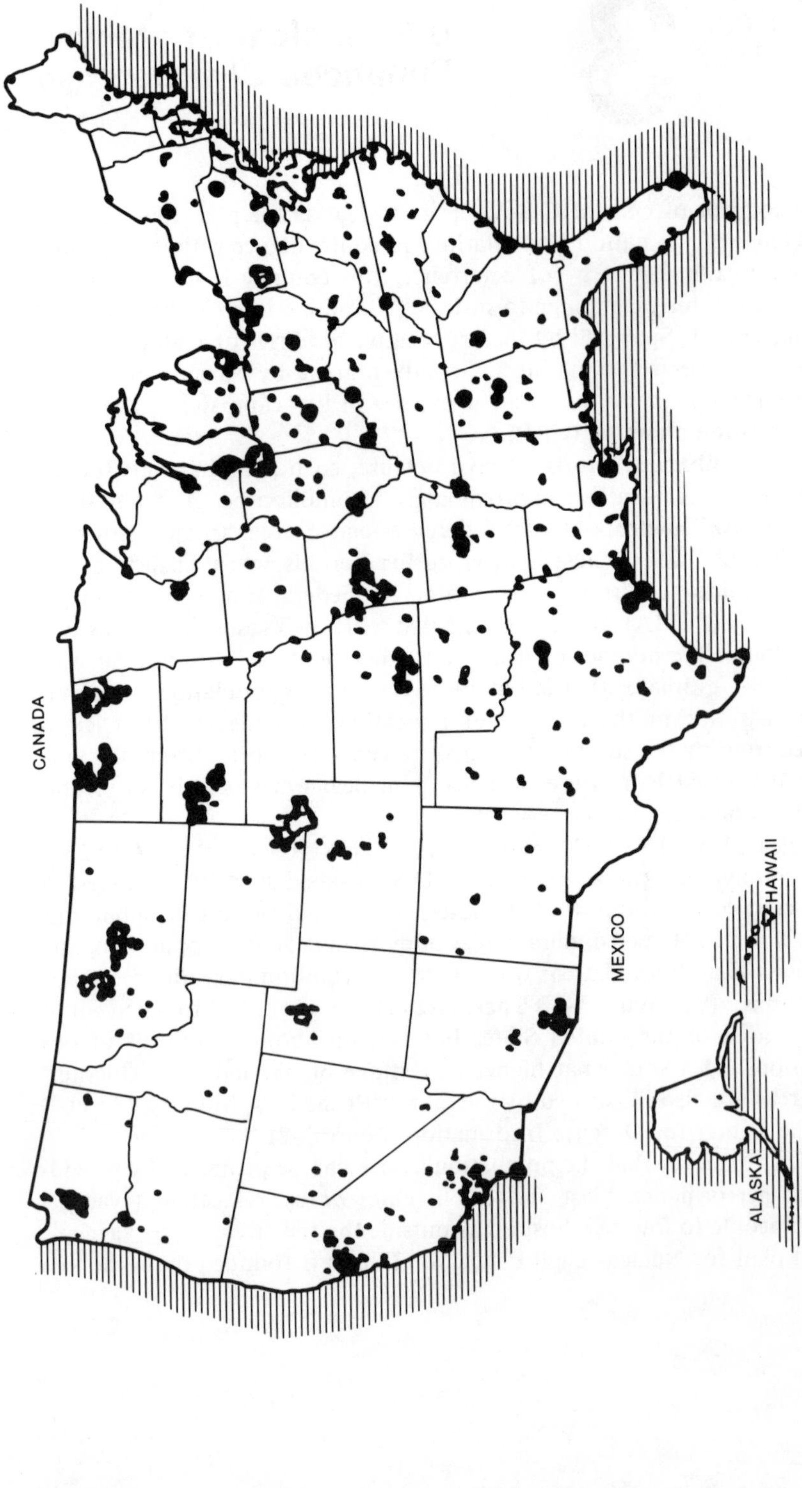

Source: Federal Emergency Management Agency (FEMA), *U.S. Crisis Relocation Planning,* February 1981.

Figure 3–1. High Risk Areas

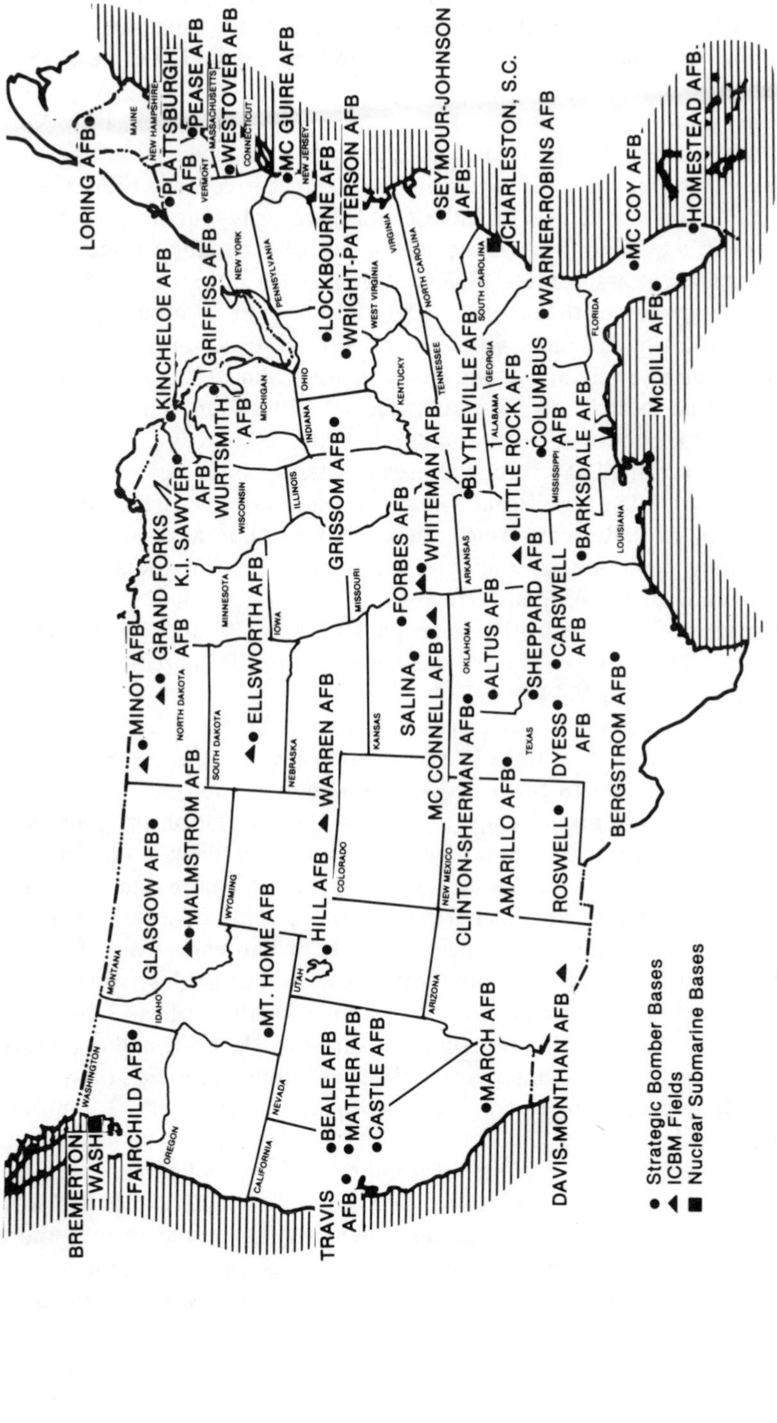

From *The Defense Monitor,* vol. 5, No. 5, July 1976, p. 3.

Figure 3–2. Prime U.S. Military Targets

options.[5] Yet, because of its awareness of the cost of blast shelters (about $70 billion) and because of its conviction that "tens of millions can be saved by evacuation," FEMA seeks to achieve a "nationwide capability for crisis relocation" pursuant to policy enunciated in Presidential Directive 41 (September 1978).

Even under the conditions of the heaviest possible attack, FEMA expects that "95 percent of our land would escape untouched, except possibly by radioactive fallout."[6] If its assumptions are correct, the FEMA argument minimizes the effects of fallout and disregards long-term ecological effects. In fact, in another recent assessment of evacuation effectiveness, FEMA arrives at a substantially less optimistic set of expectations. Here, FEMA acknowledges that if the Soviet Union "were to mount an all-out attack on the United States with their present strategic forces, taking into account accuracy, reliability, and other factors, almost the whole population would be located less than 100 miles of at least one nuclear detonation." Indeed, about half the population would be in areas experiencing at least "light damage" (overpressure greater than 1 pound per square inch). (See table 3–1.) The significance of these expectations, as FEMA recognizes, is that virtually every American would be within range of potentially deadly fallout radiation exposure and about half the U.S. population would be involved in direct weapons effects.[7]

The idea of crisis relocation dates back to the 1950s and was given particularly visible endorsement by the Defense Civil Preparedness Agency (now merged into FEMA) in 1977.[8]

Further endorsement was provided in September 1978 by Presidential Directive 41, which also linked CRP to increased U.S. deterrence and a reduced susceptibility to Soviet crisis coercion. Yet, not until the present time has there been any attempt to support the evacuation program with significant budgetary increases. The new sense of urgency is due in large part to fears that the Soviet Union is believed to spend more than the equivalent of $2 billion annually on civil defense and that it is constructing a plan to protect 110,000 key government officials in hardened blast shelters.[9] Spurred by such fears, FEMA now seeks to do its part to close still another kind of "window of vulnerability." As of June 30, 1982, of the 3,043 crisis relocation plans required nationwide for various risk, host, and combined risk/host jurisdictions, initial plans had been completed for 798, or approximately 26 percent of requirements. These plans cover about 12.3 million risk area residents.[10]

Much of the current argument for improved U.S. civil defense via CRP flows from the assumption that the Soviets have long been concerned with such defense in their military planning and that they could recover more easily than the United States from a nuclear war. Since Soviet civil defense measures, it is alleged, might limit Soviet fatalities from a U.S. retaliation

Table 3-1
Distance from Nearest Weapons (Military-Industrial Attacks)

Distance (miles)	*Fraction of Population (percent)*
10	45
20	65
40	75
100	95
200	99

Source: FEMA calculations.

to the low tens of millions, these measures could undermine deterrence by upsetting the balance of mutual population vulnerability. What this argument ignores is that a rational Soviet adversary, in deciding whether or not a first strike would be gainful, would necessarily be unimpressed by the prospect of relative advantage, that it might emerge from a nuclear war in a better position than the United States. It would base this decision only on expectations of whether or not the result would entail unacceptable damage for itself. Even if the U.S. population were perceived as substantially more vulnerable, a Soviet first strike, in order to be cost effective, would always have to rest on the expectation that it would preclude an assuredly destructive U.S. reprisal.

There is, however, no reason to believe that the Soviet Union could entertain such an expectation. The well-known CIA study on the subject (*Soviet Civil Defense,* July 1978) notes that Soviet blast-resistant shelter space is designed to protect only 110,000 government and party leaders and that these shelters are vulnerable to direct attack. The study also points out that for the Soviets to protect the 12 to 24 percent of the total work force that would be left behind after crisis relocation, the remaining space per person in each shelter would need to be limited to between 0.5 and 1 square meter. And even if the shelters were psychologically bearable and able to survive the effects of blast, their inhabitants would stand little chance of surviving suffocation, heat, fallout, and starvation.

The attractiveness of Soviet civil defense is not significantly enhanced by even the most optimistic asumptions about blast sheltering. A study prepared by the comptroller general of the United States on August 5, 1981, notes that Soviet civil defense "does provide thousands of blast resistant shelters which could protect up to 13 million people from the initial effects of a nuclear attack." It goes on to indicate, however, that "The ability to survive the initial effects does not ensure survival against radioactive fallout and other long-term effects of a general nuclear war."[11]

What about those Soviet citizens who had been evacuated? Here, the promise of CRP is even more limited than it is for the United States since the Soviet Union lacks even a developed highway system that would link out-lying regions to the industrial hub. Understanding this deficiency, administration civil defense planner T.K. Jones claims that Soviet evacuation plans call for 17 million urban residents to walk 30 miles and then build expedient shelters.[12] For those who might manage such a walk, it is likely that their hastily constructed "expedient" shelters would render them even more vulnerable than those citizens who had been left behind.

The CIA study, *Soviet Civil Defense,* concludes that "Under the most favorable conditions for the USSR, including a week or more to complete urban evacuation and then to protect the evacuated population, Soviet civil defenses could reduce casualties to the low tens of millions."[13] This conclusion is based upon a scenario envisioning an attack against exclusively high-value military and economic targets. Hence, the Soviet population was not deliberately targeted and only a single U.S. retaliatory attack (immediately following the Soviet first strike) was assumed. It follows, as the report itself proceeds to indicate, that casualty levels would be far greater if (1) the U.S. attack were to take place during evacuation, (2) the attack were larger, (3) the attack were protracted and sustained, (4) the attack were directed against populations as such, (5) the evacuation were chaotic or otherwise impeded.

For example, according to studies by the U.S. Arms Control and Disarmament Agency (ACDA), even with successful evacuation of 80 percent of the urban population and best available shelters for the remaining 20 percent, the number of Soviet fatalities from *short-term effects* would still be 25 to 35 million. If the United States were to resort to ground-bursting instead of air-bursting nuclear weapons, there would be 40 to 50 million Soviet fatalities (because of the increased fallout). Moreover, if the United States were to retarget some of its nuclear weapons against the evacuated population, 70 to 85 million people would be killed in the Soviet Union.[14]

Other recent studies indicate that a U.S. nuclear retaliation would produce substantial damage to the Soviet Union even with a small number of weapons aimed at crucial targets.[15] The United States possesses substantially more weaponry and equivalent megatonnage than would be required for an exceedingly destructive nuclear retaliation against the USSR. And this is the case even when only the immediate, direct, and easily measured nuclear effects are taken into account.

Looking over the ACDA study, *An Analysis of Civil Defense in Nuclear War* (December 1978), Soviet population losses are examined after a war begun by a Soviet first strike against U.S. strategic forces, other U.S. military targets, and U.S. industry and after U.S. retaliation against a similar set of Soviet targets. A force posture is assumed in which U.S. forces are in a generated condition—a posture of alert readiness that would occur in times of tension. Considering only fatalities that would ensue from blast, radiation, and short-term fallout effects (over a longer period many additional fatalities would occur), it is apparent that casualty levels, even under the most optimistic assumptions, would be extremely high. (See figure 3–3.)

To understand the current U.S. program for CRP, we must consider that program within the context of the developing nuclear warfighting strategy of deterrence. Faced with what is perceived as a relentless buildup and refinement of Soviet strategic forces and with an adversary that is allegedly preparing for nuclear war, the United States suggests a compelling need for rejecting the principles of Mutual Assured Destruction (MAD). Discounting the idea that the Soviets can be deterred by the prospect of U.S. strategic forces that can deliver overwhelming nuclear retaliation after riding out a first-strike attack, the administration believes that deterrence now rests on likely net prowess during a nuclear war. This is not to suggest that the administration seeks a nuclear war, but that preparedness to fight such a war is believed essential to effective prevention. Building upon the foundations of Presidential Directive 59, signed by President Carter on July 25, 1980, the Reagan nuclear policy thus goes far beyond the objective of survivable and penetration-capable strategic forces to steadily accelerated preparations for nuclear warfighting. In this connection the March 1982 charter setting forth the seven-year improved civil defense program for the U.S. established a policy that "complements primary U.S. reliance on strategic offensive forces as the preponderant factor in maintaining deterrence."[16]

The rationale of U.S. nuclear policy, however, is not limited to deterrence. Anticipated by former Secretary of Defense Harold Brown's statement that "We are necessarily giving greater attention to how a nuclear war would actually be fought by both sides if deterrence fails,"[17] this policy also counsels preparations for a nuclear war that might be protracted and carefully controlled. Accepting the position that war at any level can be won or lost and that the United States must possess the ability to wage nuclear war rationally, this policy reflects the understanding that a combination of counterforce targeting (a strategy that emphasizes targeting of an adversary's military capability, especially its strategic military capability), air defense, ballistic missile defense, and crisis relocation of urban populations could make nuclear war tolerable.

In advancing these ideas, the United States has offered no evidence that the Soviets are preparing to "fight and win" a nuclear war, if by this assessment we mean that they are preparing to strike first.[18] Rather, all of the evidence suggests that the USSR, in response to any use of nuclear weapons by the United States, would employ the full range of its nuclear options—

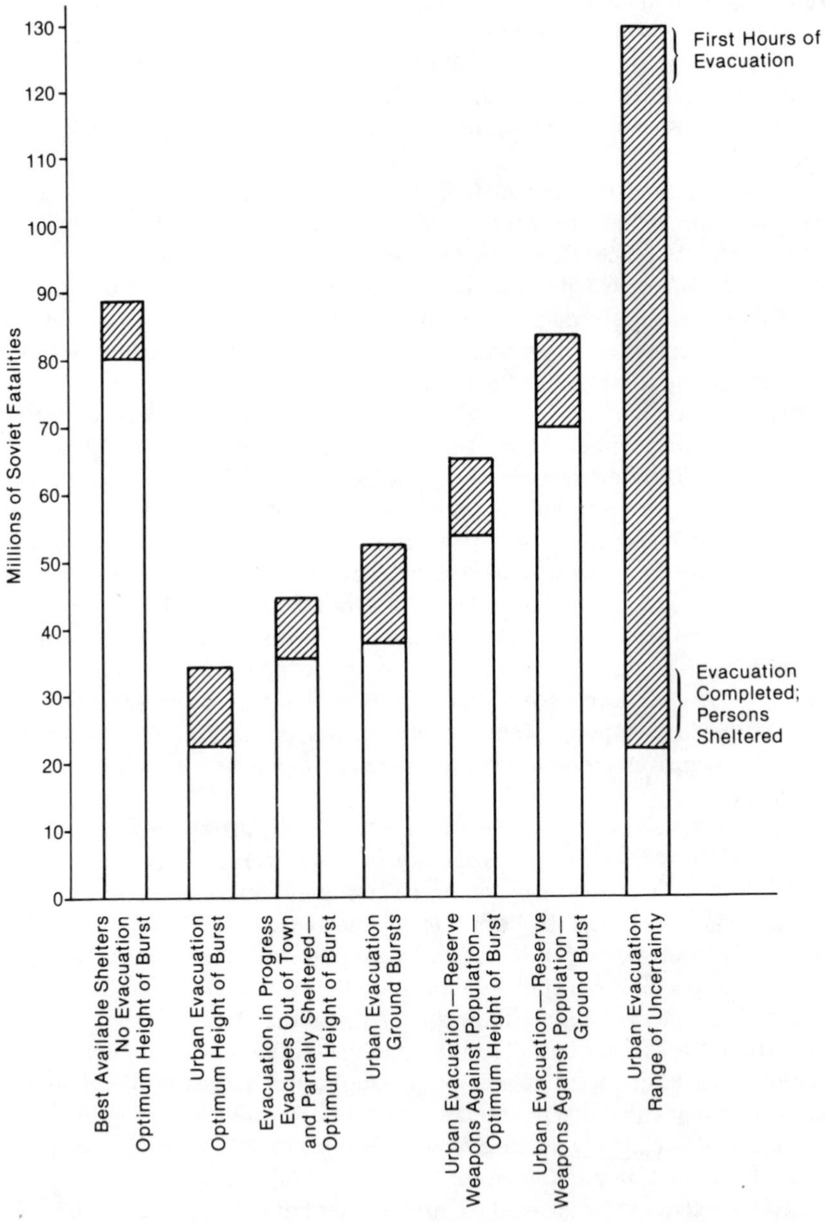

Source U.S. Arms Control and Disarmament Agency, *An Analysis of Civil Defense in Nuclear War* (Washington, D.C.: ACDA, December 1978), p. 12.

Figure 3-3. Sensitivity of Immediate Fatalities to Attack Assumptions (U.S. Forces Generated)

that it would not engage in the kind of limited nuclear war envisioned by current U.S. strategic policy. Indeed, Soviet spokesmen (apparently aware of the limits of Soviet civil defense just discussed) continue to advance the argument that any nuclear war would be intolerable and that there would be no purpose in fighting and winning such a war.

In a speech before the twenty-sixth Congress of the Soviet Communist party on February 23, 1981, Leonid Brezhnev said, "To try and outstrip each other in the arms race, or to expect to win a nuclear war, is dangerous madness." In a speech at a Kremlin rally on November 6, 1981, Marshall Dmitri F. Ustinov, Minister of Defense, stated, "Western politicians and strategists stubbornly push the thesis that Soviet military doctrine assumes the possibility of an 'initial disarming strike,' of survival, and even of victory, in a nuclear war. All this is a deliberate lie." And in an address at a Soviet–American seminar in Washington on January 12, 1982, Nikolai N. Inozemtsev, Director of the Soviet Institute of World Economy and International Relations, observed, "Political and military doctrines have been changed. This has been reflected in our internal life. There is a new determination to seek sharp reductions."

A natural complement to the developing nuclear warfighting strategy of deterrence embraced by the United States, the plan for CRP is founded upon the Carter administration's Presidential Directive 41. The 1978 directive sought to improve deterrence by increasing the number of Americans who could survive a nuclear attack through evacuation. It was also intended to ensure greater continuity of government in the event that deterrence were to fail, an objective reinforced by the provisions of PD-58 (August 1980) outlining relocation plans for leading federal officials during times of crisis.

There are, however, significant differences between the Carter and Reagan plans for relocation. With its release of National Security Decision Directive 26 in March 1982, the Reagan administration went far beyond PD-41 in terms of the scope and substance of U.S. civil defense. In contrast to PD-41, NSDD-26 represents a clear commitment to a national policy of making nuclear war more thinkable and calls for "the survival of a substantial portion of the American people in the event of a nuclear attack." In this connection, the Reagan directive envisions survival in a "protracted" nuclear war. According to Louis O. Giuffrida, FEMA director, on October 9, 1981, "The other thing this administration has categorically rejected is the short-war, mutually assured destruction, it'll all be over in 20 minutes so why the hell mess around spending dollars on it. [sic] We're trying to inject long-war mentality."[19]

Whether the war is expected to be long or short, FEMA officials assume that the United States would have several days to a week to evacuate the so called high-risk areas during a period of rising international tensions. Discounting the prospect of a surprise attack, this assumption stipulates

Soviet conformance to this country's rules in beginning a nuclear war. Such a stipulation, however, is not informed by pertinent evidence. Nor is it consistent with Department of Defense (DOD) assumptions, since the Pentagon continues to base strategic requirements on the expectation of a "no warning" attack. It is *this* expectation that provides the rationale for accelerated U.S. improvement and expansion of strategic forces.

Another administration assumption underlying CRP is that a government-directed civilian evacuation plan in the face of a nuclear war would not degenerate into chaos. Analogizing CRP to movement in rush hour traffic, FEMA suggests, "It is a difficult and complex problem requiring much planning, but it is possible. After all, we relocate millions of workers from our big cities every evening rush hour. We have moved hundreds of thousands to safety in time of hurricane or flood. And in a case like this, it could save as many as 100 million lives. It would be an orderly, controlled evacuation. Your own local authorities would give detailed instructions through radio, television and the press, telling you what necessities to take along [See figure 3–4, Checklist of Supplies], what arrangements have been made for transportation—by bus, train, or private car—where you will find safety in a small town or rural host area, and what routes to follow to get there."[20]

Ignoring critical differences that exist between natural disasters and a nuclear attack, FEMA offers no evidence in support of such plans. In an assessment of the relocation option offered in *Nuclear Weapons,* a recent report of the secretary-general of the United Nations:

> Evacuation of population from areas expected to come under attack has to be planned very carefully in advance. Apart from transportation and housing of evacuees, this planning must include at least short-term provisions for the relocated population. Information and instructions to the general public would have to be issued in advance. Even if instructions were available, however, the execution of an evacuation would probably be accompanied by confusion and panic. Large-scale evacuation is, therefore, in most cases, no attractive option.[21]

Further complicating FEMA plans for orderly relocation during a crisis, CRP envisions a continuation of critically needed services and essential production in the risk areas. To make such continuation possible, key workers would not be asked to remain in risk areas. Rather, "They would be advised to relocate, with their families, to nearby, closer-in host areas—from which the key workers would *commute* [emphasis in original] to their jobs on a two-shift or similar basis."[22] According to Richard Bottoroff, Director, Emergency Preparedness, District of Columbia, members of Congress are not identified as key workers.

Once successfully relocated, citizens are told to expect the following conditions by FEMA:

When you arrive, reception centers will be there to welcome you and assign you temporary housing, and special arrangements will be made to upgrade the local level of fallout protection in case the crisis should be followed by attack. In fact, we need fallout protection in place everywhere because there is no telling where it may be needed. But even if you are unable to reach a shelter, you can still improvise some protection."[23]

FEMA instructions for shelters in host areas include plans to make basement areas safer and, if no basements are available, to follow instructions for "expedient shelters." As a last resort relocated populations are advised to seek fallout protection "at the nearest public shelter."

Since people may need to remain in shelters until fallout radiation has decayed to acceptable levels, FEMA has embarked upon a program to construct and distribute "ventilation kits"—manually operated ventilation devices "to improve both total survival and the ratio of uninjured to injured survivors." These kits will be deployed by FEMA in "selected counterforce host areas."[24] As of June 1982, of the required 681 plans for counterforce areas (those areas that contain strategic offensive forces such as missiles, submarines or bombers), 344 initial plans had been completed. These plans represent about 50 percent of requirements and cover an estimated risk area population of over 7 million persons.[25] Such efforts are to be augmented by plans for "Radiological Defense Officers" (RDOs). To support this "keystone of a functioning radiological defense system," FEMA will provide "31 full time RDOs, at the State and State-area level, in the counterforce States."[26]

FEMA recognizes, however, the problematic nature of "fire survival" in residential basements. Even if the agency is correct in assuming that home basements provide a measure of blast and fallout protection, "Fire survival in residential basements will require active fire defense on the part of the basement occupants. Only above 5-psi blast overpressure, where the residence is expected to be blown clear of the basement, is fire unlikely to pose a significant threat to the survivors."[27] To maximize basement protection, host area residents are urged to "share your basement."

In the event that no basement protection is available, citizens are told to improvise fallout shelters. In this connection it is assumed that they will have followed prior instructions concerning transport of tools, especially shovels, picks, and hammers, to host areas. According to FEMA, "One fallout-protected space can be developed by moving (on the average) about one cubic yard of earth (about 70 to 100 buckets full of earth).[28] (See figure 3–5.)

The Reagan administration's major objective for CRP is "to provide for survival of a substantial portion of the U.S. population in the event of a nuclear attack preceded by strategic warning, and for continuity of government, should deterrence and escalation control fail."[29] As we have already seen, CRP also seeks, among other things, to "Enhance deterrence and

WHAT TO DO BEFORE YOU LEAVE A HIGH-RISK AREA

1. Get ample supply of any prescription medicines and special foods.
2. Collect all your important papers and package them preferably in plastic wrappers in metal container (tool box, fishing-tackle box, etc.).
3. Check home for security; see that all locks are secure; store valuables being left behind (silverware, etc.,) in a safe place.
4. Close all window blinds, shades, and drapes to help prevent fires from the heat wave of a nuclear explosion.
5. If you use your car, be sure you have enough gasoline, and prepare to take shovels, picks, hammers, and work-gloves—all will be needed to help improvise fallout shelter.
6. Stay tuned to your local TV or radio station for instructions on relocating if so directed by government officials.
7. Go over all instructions with your family so that all will understand what to do.

WHAT TO TAKE WITH YOU IN RELOCATING TO A SAFER AREA

(Take all these items if using your car. If using public transportation, take those marked "X.")

Clothing and Bedding	
☐ X work gloves	☐ X rain garments
☐ X work clothes	☐ X extra pair of shoes
☐ X extra underclothing	☐ X extra socks or stockings
☐ X outerwear (depending on season)	☐ sleeping bags and/or
	☐ blankets and sheets

Food and Utensils	
☐ Take all the food you can carry (particularly canned or dried food requiring little preparation.)	☐ eating utensils
	☐ plastic or paper plates, cups, and napkins
☐ water	☐ plastic and paper bags
☐ thermos jug or plastic bottles	☐ X candles and matches
☐ bottle and can opener	☐ plastic drop cloth

Source: Taken from DCPA, *Protection in the Nuclear Age*, pp. 50–51; reprinted as "Survival Supplies" in Hearing, "FEMA Oversight", p. 90.

Figure 3-4. U.S. Government's Checklist of Personal Supplies for Survival

Personal, Safety, Sanitation and Medical Supplies

- ☐ X Battery operated (transistor) radios, extra batteries
- ☐ X flashlight, extra batteries
- ☐ X soap
- ☐ X shaving articles
- ☐ X sanitary napkins
- ☐ X detergent
- ☐ X towels and washcloths
- ☐ X toilet paper
- ☐ emergency toilet
- ☐ garbage can
- ☐ newspapers
- ☐ first aid kit
- ☐ X special medication (insulin, heart tablets, or other)
- ☐ X toothbrush and toothpaste

Baby Supplies

- ☐ X diapers
- ☐ X bottles and nipples
- ☐ X milk or formula
- ☐ X powder
- ☐ X rubber sheeting, etc.

Tools for Constructing a Fallout Shelter

- ☐ pick ax
- ☐ shovel
- ☐ saw
- ☐ hammer
- ☐ broom
- ☐ ax
- ☐ crowbar
- ☐ nails and screws
- ☐ screw driver
- ☐ wrench

Important Papers

- ☐ X Social Security Card
- ☐ X Deeds
- ☐ X Insurance Policies
- ☐ X Stocks and Bonds
- ☐ X Will
- ☐ X Saving Accounts Books
- ☐ X Credit Cards and Currency

WHAT NOT TO TAKE WITH YOU IN RELOCATING TO SAFER AREA

Do not Take

- ☐ FIREARMS—(guns of any kind)
- ☐ NARCOTICS
- ☐ ALCOHOL BEVERAGES

"FALLOUT PROTECTION IS DIRT CHEAP"

MEANING, FALLOUT PROTECTION CAN BE DEVELOPED *DURING A CRISIS* BY:

- **ADDING EARTH BESIDE AND ON TOP OF STRUCTURES WHICH TODAY DO NOT PROVIDE SUFFICIENT FALLOUT PROTECTION**
- **CONSTRUCTING EXPEDIENT SHELTERS**

ONE FALLOUT—PROTECTED SPACE CAN BE DEVELOPED BY MOVING (ON THE AVERAGE) ABOUT ONE CUBIC YARD OF EARTH (ABOUT 70 to 100 BUCKETS FULL OF EARTH)

Source: Taken from FEMA, *Materials for Presentation on Nuclear Civil Protection,* P & P-2, September 1980.

Figure 3–5. Advice on Protection from Fallout

stability in conjunction with our strategic offensive and other strategic defensive forces. Civil defense, as an element of the strategic balance, should assist in maintaining perceptions that this balance is favorable to the U.S.''[30] This objective stems from the belief that a more survivable U.S. population would reduce the likelihood that this country could be coerced in time of crisis. Confronted with large-scale civil defense upgrading in the United States, Soviet perceptions of a decreasingly vulnerable U.S. population would—in Soviet cost-benefit calculations of alternative courses of action—allegedly reduce the expected benefits of ''escalation dominance.''

In basing CRP upon such assumptions, FEMA and the administration neglect some important considerations. (1) It is by no means clear that CRP would in fact reduce U.S. population vulnerability, or that, even if it would, the Soviet Union would perceive such a reduction. Leaving aside the hazards of fallout, there is no reason to assume Soviet inability or unwillingness to target relocated populations. And it cannot be misunderstood that in order to save lives, evacuation would need to be augmented with effective plans for the provision of food, water, medical care and supplies, sanitation, security, and filtered air. (2) It is clear that CRP would be of no survival benefit in the event of a Soviet bolt-from-the-blue surprise attack, an attack that FEMA regards as the least likely scenario but that the Soviets (as recognized by DOD plans) might well regard as most rational under certain conditions (e.g., Soviet expectations of an imminent U.S. first strike). (3) U.S. resort to CRP would almost certainly be viewed as a provocative act by the Soviet Union, perhaps even confirming their oft-stated fears of a U.S. first strike. Such fears have already been heightened by the expanded U.S. development of plans for fighting a protracted nuclear war and for associated counterforce weapons systems (MX, MK-12A RV, Trident II). Still other fear-inducing measures undertaken by the United States include the deployment of a new generation of intermediate-range nuclear missiles in selected NATO countries, the administration's rejection of a genuine nuclear freeze, and the U.S. refusal to parallel Soviet renunciation of the right to first use of nuclear weapons. (4) CRP would have no effect on Soviet calculations of the expected cost of striking first since it would have no bearing on the survivability and penetration capability of U.S. strategic forces. Even if an enormous survival asymmetry were to develop between the United States and the Soviet Union, the Soviet inclination to coerce or to strike first would be unaffected by its relative lack of vulnerability. This is the case because the rationality of preemption depends not on expectations of comparative suffering but only on expectations of avoiding or reducing assuredly destructive retaliation. (5) All of the alleged benefits of CRP hinge on the judgment that a superpower nuclear war would be carefully controlled and cooperative, that there would be a ''ladder of escalation'' rather than spasmodic exchanges. (6) CRP provides false reassurance to the American people, encouraging the very processes of denial that make nuclear war increasingly likely.

Perhaps the most flawed assumption of CRP is that relocated populations could expect a better chance to survive. In the absence of normally functioning health-care delivery systems, people with chronic illnesses would be especially vulnerable, while fractures, burns, and lacerations would go untreated. Coupled with greatly heightened incidence of both disease and psychological trauma, medical problems would be aggravated by the overwhelming number of rotting corpses. According to the distinguished physician, Herbert L. Abrams:

> The health threat created by millions of postattack corpses is a serious one. In many areas radiation levels will be so high that corpses will remain untouched for weeks on end. With transportation destroyed, survivors weakened, and a multiplicity of post-shelter reconstruction tasks to be performed, corpse disposal will be remarkably complicated. In order to bury the dead, an area 5.7 times as large as the city of Seattle would be required for the cemetery.[31]

Writing in the November 1981 issue of the *New England Journal of Medicine,* Dr. Abrams and Dr. William E. Von Kaenel examined the effects of a 6559-megaton attack on the United States (the so-called CRP-2B models used by FEMA in civil defense planning). Representing, in terms of yield, the equivalent of 524,720 Hiroshima bombs, such an attack could be expected to have the following consequences:

> Moments after the attack, 86 million people—nearly 40 percent of the population—will be dead. An additional 34 million—27 percent of the survivors—will be severely injured. Fifty million additional fatalities are anticipated during the shelter period, for a total of 133 million deaths. Many of the millions of surviving injured will have received moderate to high radiation doses. Approximately 60 million may survive and emerge from the shelter period without serious injury and with relatively limited radiation exposure.[32]

It should be apparent from these assessments that the United States has been thinking against itself. Rather than accept the informed understanding that a nuclear war with the Soviet Union would totally shatter the fabric of American life, our leaders have decided instead to presume that such a war might be tolerably sustained. Nurtured by the facile tenets of realpolitik, this presumption contributes not to security, but to the predatory embrace of collective disintegration.

In *The Plague,* Camus tells us: "At the beginning of the pestilence and when it ends, there's always a propensity for rhetoric. . . . It is in the thick of a calamity that one gets hardened to the truth—in other words, to silence." As long as we continue to stand in the ruins of thought, ruins created by the desolate clairvoyance of civil defense planners, we will be unable to avoid the more tangible ruins of a nuclear war. Without a full awareness of the futility of relocation, we will be imprisoned within the lethal interstices of a sinister technology, unable to convert the angst of our time into a relentless search for life.

Maurice Merleau-Ponty's *Phénoménologie de la Perception* bring us back to the origin of the problem, the human incapacity to grasp meaning before or after life: "Neither my birth nor my death can appear to me as *my* experiences. . . . I can only grasp myself as "already born" and "still living"—grasping my birth and death only as pre-personal horizons." Again, although some repression of the fear of death may be essential to happiness and well-being, it can—where it is too successful—make extinction more imminent. Understood in terms of the American imperative to avoid nuclear war, this suggests that we must learn to identify such war with the cessation of life. By rejecting the humiliating delusions that blind our leaders to lucidity, we can replace the rarified gibberish of realpolitik with a language and policy of reason and promise.

Notes

1. See FEMA document, *U.S. Crisis Relocation Planning,* Washington, D.C., February 1981.
2. See Toby Moffett, Chairman, Environment, Energy and Natural Resources Subcommittee of the Committee on Government Operations, U.S. House of Representatives, Opening Statement at Hearing, "FEMA Oversight: Will U.S. Nuclear Attack Evacuation Plans Work?" 97th Cong. 2d sess., April 22, 1982, p. 1.
3. From FEMA, *U.S. Crisis Relocation Planning.*
4. Ibid.
5. See FEMA, *Local Government Emergency Planning,* CPG 1-8, April 1982, pp. 5-6.
6. From FEMA film on nuclear preparedness, screened before a Hearing of a Subcommittee of the Committee on Government Operations, U.S. House of Representatives, April 22, 1982, pp. 5-6 of Hearing Record.
7. See FEMA, *Attack Environment Manual,* chapter 1, Introduction to Nuclear Emergency Operations, CPG 2-1A1, May 1982, panel 14.
8. See Defense Civil Preparedness Agency, Department of Defense, U.S. Government, *Protection in the Nuclear Age,* Washington, D.C., February 1977, p. 49.
9. See assessment made by the U.S. Department of Defense, *Soviet Military Power,* n.d., published in 1982, p. 69.

10. See FEMA Director Louis O. Guiffrida, *FEMA Annual Report 1981, A Report to the President on Comprehensive Emergency Management,* p. 3.

11. See Report to the Congress of the United States, *Countervailing Strategy Demands Revision of Strategic Force Acquisition Plans,* U.S. General Accounting Office, MASAD-81-35, August 5, 1981, p. 9.

12. See T.K. Jones, *Industrial Survival and Recovery after a Nuclear Attack: A Report to the Joint Committee on Defense Production,* U.S. Congress (Seattle: The Boeing Aerospace Company, November 1976).

13. See CIA, *Soviet Civil Defense,* p. 4.

14. See statement by ACDA Deputy Director Keeny before the Senate Committee on Banking, Housing and Urban Affairs: Civil Defense, January 8, 1979, 95th Cong. 2d sess., reprinted in ACDA, *Documents on Disarmament,* June 1982.

15. See Geoffrey Kemp, "Nuclear Forces for Medium Powers, parts II and III. Strategic Requirements and Options," Adelphi Papers 107, London: International Institute for Strategic Studies, 1974; The Metis Corporation, "Data Base and Damage Criteria for Measurement of Arms Limitation Effects on War Supporting Industry," Contract no. ACDA/WEC-242, Alexandria, Va.: Metis Corporation, June 1974; and U.S. Arms Control and Disarmament Agency, *An Analysis of Civil Defense in Nuclear War* (Washington, D.C.: ACDA, December 1978).

16. See FEMA News Release no. 82–26, March 30, 1982.

17. See Harold Brown, Remarks delivered at the Convocation Ceremonies for the 97th Naval War College Class, Newport, R.I., August 20, 1980, p. 6.

18. Of course, current U.S. civil defense policy is premised on the assumption that there will be no sudden Soviet first-strike—a bolt-from-the-blue attack. Moreover, much of current U.S. nuclear strategy is based on the plausibility of limited nuclear war, an idea that contradicts the assessment that the Soviets are making plans to "fight and win" a nuclear war.

19. See "President Reagan's Civil Defense Program," *The Defense Monitor,* vol. 11, no. 5, 1982, Center for Defense Information, Washington, D.C., p. 3.

20. See Hearing, "FEMA Oversight," p. 7.

21. See *Nuclear Weapons,* A Report of the Secretary-General (Brookline, Mass.: Autumn Press, 1980), p. 102, published with the authorization of the United Nations.

22. See *Materials for Presentation on Nuclear Civil Protection,* FEMA, P & P-2, September 1980.

23. See Hearing, "FEMA Oversight," p. 7.

24. See FEMA, *A New Impetus: Emergency Management for Attack Preparedness,* FEMA-1/June 1980, p. 5.

25. See FEMA, *Annual Report 1981,* p. 3.

26. Ibid. See also, FEMA, *Radiological Defense Preparedness,* SM 5.2., February 1981; FEMA, *Guide for the Design and Development of a Local Radiological Defense Support System,* CPG 1–30, June 1981; and FEMA, *Decontamination Considerations,* For Architects and Engineers, TR-71, April 1980.

27. See FEMA, *Attack Environment Manual,* chapter 3, What the Planner Needs to Know about Blast and Shock, CPG 2–1A3, May 1982, panel 29.

28. See figure 3–5 with FEMA's optimistic slogan, "Fallout Protection Is Dirt Cheap." Pursuant to order of the president, FEMA has scheduled courses in fallout shelter analysis to prepare military and civilian personnel for maximizing fallout shelter in various kinds of structures. Successful completion of this course by qualified persons carries FEMA certification as a fallout shelter analyst. See FEMA, *Announcement of 1982 Courses in Fallout Shelter Analysis,* L-90, January 1982.

29. See FEMA, News Release no. 82-26, March 30, 1982.

30. Ibid.

31. See Herbert L. Abrams, "Infection and Communicable Diseases," in Ruth Adams and Susan Cullen, eds., *The Final Epidemic: Physicians and Scientists on Nuclear War* (Chicago: Educational Foundation for Nuclear Science, 1981), p. 201.

32. See "Special Report: Medical Problems of Survivors of Nuclear War," *New England Journal of Medicine,* November 12, 1981, p. 1226.

4 U.S. Nuclear Strategy: Proliferation

The current U.S. position on strategy and arms control must also be considered from the perspective of nuclear proliferation[1] to other states. Reflecting the principles of realpolitik thinking, this position now hastens the portent of nuclear war involving not only the superpowers, but also states that have yet to acquire the instruments of atomic destruction. The time is opportune, therefore, for a systematic look at the particular risks of nuclear proliferation that accrue from a continuing adherence to geopolitics.

The Reagan administration's initial assessment that nuclear proliferation can be regarded with equanimity rested more on a pessimistic view of successful control than on an optimistic view of a world of multiplying nuclear powers. Yet among the community of international relations scholars, strategic theorists, and atomic scientists, nuclear proliferation has always had its ardent supporters. Today, as in the past, certain members of this community continue to favor the spread of nuclear weapons and nuclear explosive capabilities on the assumption that it would produce security by enlarging the number of states with credible deterrence postures. This view of nuclear proliferation is often referred to as the "porcupine theory" because it suggests that a nuclear weapons state can walk like a porcupine through the forests of international affairs—that is, that it can presume safety.

Such thinking has been with us for a long time. Winston Churchill clearly had a porcupine argument in mind when he made the following statement before the House of Commons on November 3, 1953:

> When I was a schoolboy, I was not good at arithmetic, but I have since heard it said that certain mathematical quantities, when they pass through infinity, change their signs from plus to minus—or the other way round. It may be that this rule may have a novel application and that when the advance of destructive weapons enables everyone to kill everybody else, nobody will want to kill anyone at all.[2]

During the 1960s General Pierre Gallois of the French Air Force wrote widely in advocacy of porcupine reasoning in nuclear strategy. The principal lines of his argument suggest that any nuclear weapons state, whatever its size and power, can be secure against aggression as long as it can deliver overwhelmingly destructive retaliation. According to Gallois: "If every nuclear power held weapons truly invulnerable to the blows of the other, the resort to force by the one to the detriment of the other would be impossible." Therefore,

> Because the risks of nuclear war cannot be compared with the benefits that might be obtained from armed conflict, because it is impossible to endure the shock and to continue with an organized military effort (and therefore impossible to envisage an armed encounter), it is necessary to make nuclear deterrence the foundation of defense policy.[3]

These views of nuclear proliferation are remarkably misconceived. Nuclear weapons states are not porcupines, and the global political system is not a forest. The tremendous power of destruction that accompanies a nuclear weapons capability does not necessarily bestow safety from attack. Indeed, it may even undercut such safety. For reasons that shall now be made clear, it is essential that policy makers in the U.S. and throughout the world look upon proliferation with unequivocal opposition.

The Belief Problem of Nuclear Deterrence

The acquisition of nuclear weapons does not automatically signal a credible deterrence posture. Unless a state is believed willing to use its nuclear weapons for retaliation, a would-be aggressor may not be deterred. And in a world of many nuclear powers, prospective aggressor states might have significant doubts about the willingness of certain other states to retaliate with nuclear arms.

One must also consider the possibility of misperception. Even if every nuclear weapons state in the proliferated system were actually willing to make good on its threat to resort to nuclear retaliation, prospective aggressor states might fail to perceive this willingness in certain instances. Here, nuclear deterrence could fail in spite of the fact that every nuclear state had in fact committed itself to nuclear threat fulfillment.

The Capability Problem of Nuclear Deterrence

We see, therefore, that a nuclear weapons state, in order to have a credible nuclear deterrence posture, must give the impression that it is willing to use its capability for nuclear retaliation. Before it can attempt to satisfy this requirement, however, the nuclear weapons state must demonstrate that it actually has such a capability. To do this, it must demonstrate more than the mere possession of nuclear retaliatory forces. It must also demonstrate the security of these forces from a first-strike attack.

Yet, although secure nuclear forces are a sine qua non of a credible nuclear deterrence posture, such forces cannot be assured among new members of the nuclear club. The superpowers have invested many years and vast amounts of money in securing their triad forces. Moreover, even these states now fear for the safety of their primary deterrent forces, a fear that may lead to real corrosion of safeguards on command and control systems.

New nuclear weapons states cannot hope to duplicate even the problematic level of force security achieved by the superpowers. Few if any such states could hope to create a diversified and expensive system involving hardening, mobility, dispersion, and multiple, complementary surveillance and early warning capabilities. In response to the resultant vulnerability of their nuclear forces, these new nuclear powers will be faced with a constant incentive to preempt. The combined effect of such incentives would be a condition of extreme instability for each new nuclear weapons state.

Once again, there is also the problem of misperception. Even if all of the new nuclear powers were actually able to maintain secure nuclear retaliatory forces, prospective aggressors might, through errors in information, perceive insecurity. Here, nuclear deterrence could fail in spite of the fact that each new nuclear power had "succeeded" in protecting its nuclear retaliatory forces.

To guard against preemption, new nuclear powers are apt to turn to strategies that pose additional hazards. These strategies will most likely involve the attachment of hair-trigger launch mechanisms to nuclear weapons systems, and/or the adoption of launch-on-warning measures, possibly with predelegations of launch authority. Even if such strategies could succeed in producing security from disarming first-strike attacks, they would surely increase the likelihood of accidental or unauthorized use of nuclear weapons.

Moreover, the spread of such strategies would affect the likelihood of nuclear war between the United States and the Soviet Union. There are at least two reasons for this judgment:

First, the generally greater likelihood of certain forms of nuclear war associated with such strategies implies an increase in the number of particular conflicts that might involve superpower participation. This is especially true if the initial nuclear conflict were to involve an ally of one or both of the superpowers.

Second, with the steady increase in the number of nuclear powers, it is conceivable that a new nuclear weapons state could launch its nuclear weapons against one or the other superpower without the victim knowing for certain where the attack originated. In the event that the victim state were to conclude that the attack came from the other superpower, a full-scale nuclear war between the United States and the Soviet Union might ensue. In such a case the new nuclear power—possibly as a result of its own inadequate system of command and control—will have catalyzed nuclear war between the superpowers.

Multiple Nuclear Arms Races

The effort to create and maintain secure nuclear retaliatory forces will generate relentless pressures for a systemwide nuclear arms race. In response to these pressures, the new nuclear weapons states will begin to engage in increasingly intense forms of qualitative and quantitative nuclear arms competition with each other. The net effect of such competition can only be a greatly heightened risk of nuclear war.

In the bad dream of living in a nuclear crowd, the nightmarish qualities would have myriad sources:

> The expanded number of nuclear powers would wreak havoc upon the already precarious idea of a stable balance of terror in world politics. There would simply be too many "players," too much ambiguity, for any sense of "balance" to be meaningful.
>
> The expanded number of nuclear powers would continue to shatter the symmetry of strategic doctrine between nuclear weapons states. Some of the new nuclear powers would shape their strategies along the lines of "minimum deterrence" or "assured destruction" capabilities. Others would seek more ambitious objectives, including a nuclear war-fighting or counterforce capability. As a result nuclear weapons might lose entirely their role as instruments of deterrence, a loss that would surely be accelerated by the first actual use of nuclear weapons by a secondary nuclear power.
>
> The expanded number of nuclear powers would ultimately create the conditions whereby first-strike attacks could be unleashed with impunity, whatever the condition of the intended victim's willingness to retaliate or the security of its retaliatory forces. This is the case because in a world of many nuclear powers, it would become possible for a nuclear-armed agressor to launch its weapons against another state without being identified. Unable to know for certain where the attack originated, the victim state might lash out blindly. In the resulting conflagration, even a worldwide nuclear war might ensue.
>
> The expanded number of nuclear powers would create the conditions for a chain reaction of nuclear exchanges. Even before it becomes pos-

sible to launch a nuclear strike anonymously, a strategic exchange might take place between two or more new nuclear weapons states that are members of opposing alliances. Ultimately, if the parties to such a clash involve clients of either or both superpowers, the ensuing chain reaction might consume the United States and the Soviet Union along with much of the rest of the world.

The expanded number of nuclear powers would create the conditions whereby nuclear weapons capabilities might be transferred to insurgent groups. A possible outcome of such microproliferation might be not only nuclear terrorism, but also an anonymous terrorist detonation that could be mistakenly blamed upon another state by the attack victim. In this way microproliferation could actually spark regional or systemwide nuclear war between states.

The expanded number of nuclear powers would create major inequalities in power between rival states. Where one rival would find itself in possession of nuclear weapons, and another rival would be denied such possession, the new nuclear state might find itself with an overwhelming incentive to strike. The net effect of such inequalities of power would be an increased probability of nuclear aggression against non-nuclear states.

Accidental Nuclear War and Nuclear Weapons Accidents

The expanded number of nuclear weapons states would increase the likelihood of accidental nuclear war. We have already seen that the reason for this is not simply a function of number (i.e., the more nuclear weapons states, the greater the number of existing risks), but it is also a consequence of the need to compensate for vulnerable nuclear forces by using risky command/control measures. In addition, all of the new nuclear powers are unlikely to invest the time and expense needed to equip the nuclear weapons themselves with appropriate safety mechanisms.

Proliferation also suggests the specter of catastrophic accidents that do not give rise to nuclear war but that still produce a nuclear yield. Since even the American record of broken arrows or nuclear weapons accidents has included a number of very close calls, one cannot help but anticipate a new rash of broken arrows among forces of new nuclear powers. What will happen when their bombers crash; when the nuclear payloads they carry are accidentally dropped or intentionally jettisoned; or when these nuclear bombs or missiles are burned in a fire on the ground? With the proliferation of nuclear weapons, such accidents can be expected to occur at an increased rate.

Unauthorized Use of Nuclear Weapons

As with accidental nuclear war and nuclear weapons accidents, nuclear proliferation would also increase the probability of the unauthorized use of nuclear weapons. This is the case, again, not only because of the expanded number of existing risks, but because the new nuclear powers would almost certainly lack the safeguards now in place in superpower arsenals. In response to the need for a quick-reaction nuclear force that can be fielded as soon as possible, new nuclear powers will inevitably turn to automatic or nearly automatic systems of nuclear retaliation that are not "encumbered" by complex and costly command/control checks.

Irrational Use of Nuclear Weapons

A final reason why the spread of nuclear weapons signals great danger concerns the increased prospect of irrational use. The greater the number of nuclear powers, the greater the probability that irrational national leaders will have nuclear options. This is the case not only because of the increase in the number of nuclear powers as such, but because many of the new nuclear powers are apt to select their leadership elites in a fashion that precludes all forms of informed public scrutiny.

Should a new nuclear weapons state fall under the leadership of a person or persons suffering from madness, severe emotional stress, or major physiological impairment, this state might initiate nuclear first strikes against other nuclear states even though enormously destructive retaliation could be anticipated. Since the logic of nuclear deterrence is based upon the assumption of rationality—the assumption that states consistently value self-preservation more highly than any other preferences—the appearance of irrational national leaders would immobilize that logic. The strategy of nuclear deterrence would not work in the face of irrational leaders with nuclear weapons. This, of course, was one of the concerns expressed by Israel in justifying its attack on the Iraqi nuclear reactor on June 7, 1981.[4]

This fact is particularly disturbing when it is understood that instances of irrationality at national leadership levels are well known in world politics. And it is even more disturbing when it is recognized that dictatorships, which provide the most limited formal safeguards on abuses of authority and which are led by the most reckless of personality types, now greatly outnumber democratic states.

None of this should suggest, however, that the greatest danger of nuclear war arises from the possible overlap of irrationality and nuclear capability. Although the portent of such overlap is significant and must be taken very seriously, it is substantially less ominous than the threat posed by leaders who are entirely sane and rational. This is the case because the very context within which nuclear strategy decisions must be made requires ventures in escalation, risk-taking, and committal—ventures that, by their very nature, must ultimately fail. In the final analysis the national leaders who ring down the curtain on human history would probably be people who desperately wanted peace. Driven by the inexorable momentum of "logic" in the nuclear age, their doomsday judgments would be unleashed for perfectly valid reasons.

Perhaps we should call into question the very idea of sanity and rationality in the present world. Does it really make sense to identify these traits with a professed willingness to make use of the engines of megadeath? Like Adolph Eichmann, whose psychiatrist in Jerusalem pronounced him perfectly sane, the head of state who gives the order to commence nuclear warfare would, in all likelihood, act in a fashion deemed consistent with the decisional circumstances. Confronted with such a world, one wherein sanity can be reconciled with both genocide and omnicide, there can be no greater insanity than to be totally sane.

The present nonproliferation regime is founded upon a scaffolding of multilateral agreements, statutes, and safeguards. The essential elements of this scaffolding are the Statute of the International Atomic Energy Agency (IAEA) (1957); the Nuclear Test Ban Treaty (1963); the Outer Space Treaty (1967); the Treaty Prohibiting Nuclear Weapons in Latin America (1968); the Seabeds Arms Control Treaty (1972); and, of course, the Treaty on the Non-Proliferation of Nuclear Weapons (NPT), which entered into force on March 5, 1970. Since certain provisions of the NPT, especially Article VI, call for a halt in the strategic arms race between the superpowers, any new U.S.-Soviet arms control agreement must be appraised from a nonproliferation standpoint. In fact, the Strategic Arms Limitation Talks (SALT) were originally conceived, in large part, as an incentive to nonnuclear powers to accept the NPT. According to Article VI of this treaty:

> Each of the Parties to the Treaty undertakes to pursue negotiations in good faith on effective measures relating to cessation of the nuclear arms race at an early date and to nuclear disarmament, and on a treaty on general and complete disarmament under strict and effective international control.

Before the world's nonnuclear powers begin to take nonproliferation seriously, a START treaty will have to be accepted by the superpowers. In the view of the nonnuclear powers, a bargain has been struck between the superpowers and themselves requiring progressive steps toward reciprocal arms restraint by the former in exchange for nonproliferation by the latter. Although it should be clear that proliferation is inimical to the security of every state, irrespective of superpower compliance with NPT obligations, the nonnuclear states regard this bargain as the only prudent path to genuine security.

In the absence of a START treaty, it is difficult to imagine that the nonnuclear weapons states will accept their restricted condition indefinitely. Rather, they are likely to become increasingly sympathetic to the position that considers the NPT a thinly veiled trick by the superpowers to maintain their bilateral dominance of the world system. Should a new treaty fail to materialize, developing countries would almost certainly come to the general understanding that nuclear weapons, like the six-gun in the American West, are indispensable equalizers in an otherwise unbalanced "struggle for existence."

Nevertheless, President Reagan's statement on nuclear nonproliferation, announced on July 16, 1981, did nothing to indicate support for Article VI of the NPT. Although the president admitted that "Further proliferation would pose a severe threat to international peace, regional and global stability, and the security interests of the United States and other countries," he recognized no critical connection between vertical and horizontal arms control. Hence, his subsequent decisions on strategic force programs (especially the MX missile decision) which stand in fundamental contradiction to the requirements of START will also undermine the NPT. Indeed, Mr. Reagan made a bad situation even worse by his plans to deploy a ballistic missile defense (BMD) system for the protection of MX.

The deployment of BMD would surely generate a parallel Soviet deployment, which would in turn generate a mutual search for new counterforce missile capabilities. Such deployment would not only doom START but would also lead to a renunciation of the ABM treaty. It would, therefore, be widely interpreted as a particularly grievous American violation of Article VI of the NPT.

In the long run, the superpowers must undertake prodigious efforts to achieve a full-fledged transformation of their central strategic relationship. Based on the incontrovertible understanding that there is no treatment for the final epidemic of nuclear war, this transformation must embrace such elements as a strategy of minimum deterrence, a comprehensive nuclear test ban, a U.S. renunciation of first use of nuclear weapons, a joint nuclear freeze, and a joint effort at creating additional nuclear-weapon free zones. The declaratory aspects of these steps must be supported by continuing reductions in strategic weapons systems, continuing restraints in the qualitative "improvement" of strategic weapon systems, improved patterns of verification, a moratorium on peaceful nuclear explosions, and major policy changes in the European theater to eliminate all tactical and intermediate-range nuclear weapons.

Ironically, the superpowers are now heading in precisely the opposite direction. While both the United States and the Soviet Union must share in the responsibility for this deteriorating state of affairs, the Reagan administration is especially culpable. Basing its developing strategic programs on extraordinarily erroneous assumptions concerning the physical and biological effects of a nuclear holocaust, the administration now plans to spend $450 billion over the next six years in order to be able to fight different kinds of nuclear wars. Instead of informing the American people of the full-blown clinical picture that would accrue from a nuclear attack and the impotence of the medical community to offer a meaningful response, the administration now urges the public to accept nuclear war as a possibly rational instrument of national policy.

Before the superpowers can accomplish the necessary transformation of their central strategic relationship, the United States must quickly change the course of its own current arms policies. As we have already noted, this change of course must reverse the current American search for an illusory capacity to wage nuclear war rationally. This change of course must reject disquieting moves toward a "launch on warning" strategy that now augment incomprehensible additions to first-strike forces. In the absence of such changes by the United States, the cumulative effect of American strategic policy can only be a heightened Soviet incentive to preempt.

All of this is not to suggest, however, that the nonnuclear powers are concerned only about the superpowers. In fact, these nonnuclear powers are also concerned about the nuclear weapons states that are not superpowers. Strictly speaking, Article VI of the NPT calls upon these states as well as the United States and the Soviet Union to pursue an end to the nuclear arms race and to promote nuclear disarmament. To date, France and China have been particularly intransigent about curbing their own nuclear weapons programs, although China has now been admitted to full IAEA membership (the last of the nuclear weapons states to join).

By limiting the importance of nuclear weapons through far-reaching patterns of denuclearization, the nonnuclear weapons states would be offered a significant incentive not to proliferate. However, it would surely be unrealistic to believe that curtailments in existing nuclear arsenals, even if they were very substantial, would be sufficient to halt the further spread of nuclear weapons. Additional steps also need to be taken to curtail the transfer of certain commercial nuclear facilities and materials. Since access to a nuclear weapons capability now depends largely on the policies of a small group of supplier states, such policies constitute a vital element of nonproliferation efforts. In the years ahead those states that carry on international trade in nuclear facilities, technology, and materials will have to improve and coordinate their export policies.

The heart of the problem, of course, is the fact that nuclear exports, while they may contribute to the spread of nuclear weapons, are a lucrative market for a supplier state. Moreover, in certain exchanges such exports are also a crucial political lever in assuring access to oil. Recognizing the conflict in objectives between nonproliferation and a nuclear export market, the IAEA, Euratom, and the NPT treaty impose obligations on nuclear exports concerning the development of nuclear explosives. Article I of the NPT pledges the signatories "not in any way to assist, encourage, or induce any non-nuclear weapon State to manufacture or otherwise acquire nuclear weapons or other nuclear explosive devices." At the same time, Article IV of the NPT ensures that "All parties to the Treaty undertake to facilitate, and have the right to participate in, the fullest possible exchange of equipment, materials, and scientific and technological information for the peaceful uses of nuclear energy." In this connection unilateral American conditions on this country's nuclear material exports are imposed by the Nuclear Non-Proliferation Act of 1978 (NNPA).

To avoid the hazards of a worldwide plutonium economy, the United States and other suppliers must press ahead with efforts to halt the diffusion of national plutonium reprocessing and enrichment facilities. If at all possible, prohibitions on the export of sensitive technologies should be carried out on a multilateral basis. While it should be generally understood that it is in every supplier state's best interests to inhibit the spread of technologies with serious proliferation hazards, such an understanding is always contingent on the expectation of restraint by every other supplier state.

What this means, in essence, is that all supplier states can be expected to comply with the requirements of a common nuclear export policy only if they all believe that such compliance will be generally observed. From the standpoint of creating an effective consensus on nuclear exports, the problem is one of securing compliance as long as each supplier state is uncertain about the reciprocal compliance of all other supplier states. Unless each supplier state believes that its own willingness to comply is generally paralleled, it is apt to calculate that the benefits of compliance are exceeded by the costs.

To relieve this problem, two things are needed: (1) an adequate system for verification of compliance with common nuclear export policies; and (2) a system of sanctions for noncompliance in which the costs of departure from such policies are so great as to outweigh the expected benefits of export revenues. In practice, the victory of nonproliferation objectives over commercial goals will depend upon the willingness and capacity of the nuclear supplier states to exert serious political and economic pressures upon recalcitrant colleagues to conform with common policies. In the absence of such willingness and capacity, supplier states are apt to pay closer attention to their balance of payments and petroleum problems than to their long-term security interests. Such priorities would have enormously corrosive effects on the nonproliferation regime.

As long as the world system fails to provide vulnerable states with a reasonable assurance of protection against nuclear attack, such states will continue to rely on the remedy of self-help. Understood in terms of the Israeli air strike against the Iraqi nuclear reactor near Baghdad, this suggests that the real adversaries of nonproliferation are not states like Israel, which may have no effective alternative to preemption but, rather, states such as France, Italy, Canada, Switzerland, and West Germany, which have undertaken imprudent sales of nuclear technologies and materials to unstable countries.

The United States must also bear certain responsibility for nonproliferation failures. In this connection, not only has it failed to dissuade its allies from their shortsighted excursions in nuclear commerce, it has also reversed efforts by the Ford and Carter administrations to defer reprocessing of civilian fuel and the use of plutonium here and abroad. Moreover, the Reagan administration has supplied Argentina with nuclear assistance, most recently in the form of 143 tons of heavy water, despite that country's refusal to comply with international nonproliferation norms. On November 18, 1983, Argentina announced that it is now capable of enriching uranium, a capability that gives it direct access to atomic bomb material.

As with all of the other elements of its foreign policy, the Reagan administration's subordination of nonproliferation objectives to alleged considerations of power—in this case a repair of relations strained by U.S. support for Britain in the Falklands war—reflects the primacy of realpolitik. The administration should not be surprised, therefore, when its intelligence surveys reveal that 31 states, many of them engaged in long-standing regional disputes, will be able to produce nuclear weapons by the year 2000.[5] Such findings are the inevitable result of misconceived judgments of national interest.

At the same time, too much faith cannot be invested in the rules and procedures of the nonproliferation regime. In its existing form, the nonproliferation treaty, which will be reviewed for the third time in 1985, does little to assure worried states about the intentions of adversary states. To attract signatories, the NPT trades off effectiveness for obeisance to national sovereignty. Although 117 states have now acceded to the treaty, a number of states with substantial nuclear power programs have yet to accept it. A state can withdraw at any time after 90 days notice, and it may choose its own inspectors. Moreover, the NPT limits the International Atomic Energy Agency to bring to public notice any breaches of the treaty. It does not bestow upon the IAEA the power to sanction such breaches. Without the authority to look for undeclared material or for clandestine operations, the IAEA in effect conducts a limited accounting operation.

In the final analysis, however, even a greatly strengthened nonproliferation regime would be inadequate to the task at hand. Although such a regime, assisted by a more vigorous IAEA with surveillance cameras and automatic fuel-rod counting machines, would certainly be welcome, a much more basic kind of change is needed. This is a change in the underlying dynamic of fear and suspicion, a dynamic that can ultimately overcome any attempts at mechanical or technical solutions. The problem is understood best, perhaps, by the remarkable Trappist monk and scholar, Thomas Merton:

> Where there is a deep, simple, all-embracing love of man, of the created world of living and inanimate things, then there will be respect for life, for freedom, for truth, for justice and there will be humble love of God. But where there is no love of man, no love of life, then make all the laws you want, all the edicts and treaties, issue all the anathemas; set up all the safeguards and inspections, fill the air with spying satellites, and hang cameras on the moon. As long as you see your fellow man as a being essentially to be feared, mistrusted, hated and destroyed, there cannot be peace on earth.[6]

In considering the problems of proliferation from the standpoint of realpolitik and U.S. nuclear strategy, we must also examine the different forms of nuclear war that these problems may create. In this connection the consequences of a nuclear war occurring through proliferation call forth an entirely new paradigm of death, disintegration, and despair. This paradigm, born of our species' most curious technological accomplishments, expands our scope of apocalyptic imaginings to new levels. With such a paradigm we can begin to fashion a framework that allows us to understand not only gigadeath (death in the billions) but the final triumph of meaninglessness and discontinuity.

In appraising the effects of nuclear war that might arise from proliferation, we must examine major points along the spectrum of nuclear conflict possibilities. Since this includes nuclear war between the superpowers, we may begin this appraisal with a consideration of nuclear war between the United States and the Soviet Union.

Superpower Nuclear War

What, exactly, would be the consequences of a nuclear war between the superpowers? For anyone who has known or studied the effects of the atomic bombings of Hiroshima and Nagasaki, it is clear that such a war would bring not only unprecedented fatalities and injuries, but incoherence. Such incoherence would be accentuated by the impairment of symbolic immortality, a process by which individual human beings ordinarily feel that they can live on through their posterity. Because the occasion of a superpower nuclear war would represent an assault on the very idea of posterity, death would take place without rebirth and the continuity of life would yield to separation and stasis.

"In a dark time," says the poet Roethke, "the eye begins to see." The problem, however, is for us all to expand and intensify our vision before the darkness becomes total. Indeed, in the aftermath of a nuclear war between the superpowers, such darkness would be quite literal. Within weeks after an exchange involving 5,000 megatons (a megaton is the equivalent of one million tons of TNT), soot, smoke, and dust from nuclear fires and groundbursts could reduce the amount of sunlight at ground level to a few percent of what is normal. According to Carl Sagan and other authors of a recent study, presented at a conference on "The World after Nuclear War" on October 31, 1983: "An unbroken gloom would persist for weeks over the Northern Hemisphere."[7]

But this would be only the beginning. For the succeeding months, the light filtering through this pall would be unable to sustain photosynthesis. As a result there would take place a devastating impairment of the process by which plants convert sunlight to food—an impairment that would cascade through all food chains producing long-term famine.

The lack of sunlight could also produce a "harsh nuclear winter" with temperatures dropping by as much as 25 °C in inland areas. Many areas could be subject to continuous snowfall, even in the summer. In addition to killing all crops in the northern hemisphere, a nuclear war between the superpowers would freeze surface waters in the interior of continents, causing a great many animals to die of thirst.

These effects, of course, would accompany an exchange that would kill immediately approximately 1.1 billion people and injure severely the same number. Moreover, because radioactive debris in huge amounts—an estimated 225 million tons in a few days—would be carried throughout the atmosphere, exposure to radioactive fallout would be far more widespread than current U.S. government expectations suggest. And urban fires set off by the nuclear blasts would generate large amounts of deadly toxins by vaporizing the huge stockpiles of stored synthetic chemicals.

The most devastating effects would be long-term. Contrary to conclusions supported by our national leaders, the Sagan study suggests that "nuclear war probably would have a major effect on climate lasting for several years."[8] High-yield nuclear explosions would inject nitrogen oxides into the stratosphere, resulting in large reductions of the ozone layer. Since this layer screens the earth from excessive amounts of ultraviolet, this could have a marked impact on microorganisms in the soil and on aquatic life.

Although such information is just now beginning to penetrate the consciousness of interested publics throughout the world, much of it has been known for some time. In a classic work of the early 1960s, biologist Tom Stonier identified correctly the serious outbreaks of famine and disease, the ensuing shock to individuals and environment that could persist for decades, the legacy of genetic damage and the disappearance of civilization.[9] In a 1975 study titled *Long-Term Worldwide Effects of Multiple Nuclear Weapons Detonations,* a special committee of the National Research Council, National Academy of Sciences, introduced its findings with the disclaimer that "No report can portray the enormity, the utter horror which must befall the targeted areas and adjoining territories."[10]

In its report the NAS committee identified the following expected consequences of an exchange of 10,000 megatons of explosive power in the northern hemisphere (an exchange twice as large as that hypothesized by Sagan): possible temperature changes in either direction and of different magnitudes; possible major global climatic changes; contamination of foods by radionuclides; possible worldwide disease epidemics in crops and domesticated animals because of ionizing radiation; possible shortening of the length of growing seasons in certain areas; possible irreversible injury to sensitive aquatic species; possible long-term carcinogenesis due to inhalation of plutonium particles; some radiation-induced developmental anomalies in persons in utero at the time of detonations; possible increase in skin cancer incidence of about 10 percent, which could increase by as much as a factor of 3 if the ozone depletion were to rise from 50 to 70 percent; severe sunburn in temperate zones and snow blindness in northern regions in the short-term; and an increased incidence of genetic disease that would not be limited to the offspring of the exposed generation, but would extend over many generations.

In considering such informed expectations, it is important to understand that they are probably very *conservative* estimates of what would happen after a superpower nuclear war. As the NAS committee indicated, its findings do not even consider the probable social, political, and economic consequences of the hypothesized nuclear exchange. Nor do they address the probable interactions between individual effects, interactions that might be utterly unexpected and lethal. To completely understand the effects of nuclear war between the United States and the Soviet Union, we will ultimately have to go beyond the separate examinations of the consequences of blast, nuclear radiation, and thermal radiation to a full consideration of possible synergy among these consequences.

Finally, in seeking to understand and absorb the probable effects of a superpower nuclear war, we must keep in mind the prevailing assumption of our government that survival is possible. This assumption, so thoroughly at odds with the prevailing medical and scientific evidence, is nothing less than a perverse caricature of the human capacity to reason. Before any semblance of a livable species could be born from the radioactive ash of a nuclear war, a gravedigger would have to wield the forceps.

Worldwide Nuclear War

If the proliferation of nuclear weapons should lead to a nuclear war involving the exchange of tens of thousands of megatons of explosive power among several states, the world would probably experience what Nevil Shute described in his modern classic, *On the Beach.* Dwarfing even the "horrendous calamity" postulated in the National Academy of Sciences report, *Long-Term Worldwide Effects of Multiple Nuclear Weapons Detonations,* such a war would represent humankind's last and most complete holocaust. As the culmination of what Camus once described as "years of absolutely insane history," worldwide nuclear war would eradicate the very boundaries of annihilation.

On the technical side the consequences of such a nuclear war might be evaluated in terms of such dimensions as atmospheric effects, effects on natural terrestrial ecosystems, effects on managed terrestrial ecosystems and effects on the aquatic environment. At the same time, such an evaluation would probably be beside the point, since it is unlikely that any significant fraction of human beings would be left to contend with this insult to planetary life. Indeed, in contrast to the expected effects of worldwide nuclear war, the poisoning, poverty, barbarism, and genetic degeneracy of the survivors experienced after a superpower nuclear war appear relatively innocuous.

Although dispassionate, scientific examinations of the postapocalypse world are necessary, they should not obscure the essential fact that such a world would be without human populations. Hence, we must ask ourselves: "So what about atmospheric effects"? "So what about effects on natural and managed terrestrial ecosystems"? "And what about effects on the aquatic environment"? If we aren't even going to be around in such a world, a world that would deny us even our posterity, what purpose can there be to scrutinizing its other properties?

In asking these questions, we must learn to understand that a systemwide nuclear war would eliminate *all* possibilities for a new beginning, for a general rebirth, for improved social and spiritual forms. Robert Lifton has written insightfully about the idea of the survivor as a creator, as one who can fashion a new self and world because he has known terrible disruption.[11] This idea loses all of its promise in a world bereft of people. Since a worldwide nuclear war would deprive us of even the energizing qualities of survivors, there would be no continuity, no learning from lessons of the past. Those who have known "the end" would take that knowledge with them. As the final legacy of realpolitik, there would be no hope.

Two-Country Nuclear War

As a result of nuclear weapons spread, an increasing number of antagonistic pairs of countries might engage in nuclear conflict. What, in fact, would be the consequences of such wars?

To answer this question with precision, of course, we would need to stipulate the kinds of weapons used, their yields, their altitudes of detonation, the prevailing weather patterns, and more. In general, however, we can say that two-country nuclear war could involve the exchange of anywhere between several Hiroshima-yield weapons (in the neighborhood of 10–20 kilotons) and several dozen ballistic missiles carrying warhead yields of up to 20 megatons each.

From what we already know about Hiroshima and the probable effects of nuclear war between the superpowers, it is evident that even the most "limited" nuclear exchange would spell catastrophe for combatant parties. The immediate effects of the explosions—thermal radiation, nuclear radiation, and blast damage—would cause wide swaths of death and destruction. Victims would be horribly injured by flash and flame burns. Retinal burns could occur in the eyes of persons at distances of several hundred miles from the explosion. People would be crushed by collapsing buildings or torn by flying glass. Others would fall victim to raging firestorms and conflagrations. Fallout injuries would include whole-body radiation injury, produced by penetrating, hard gamma radiation; superficial radiation burns produced by soft radiations; and injuries produced by the deposition of radioactive substances within the body.

In the aftermath, medical facilities that might still exist would be taxed beyond endurance. Water supplies would become unusable as a result of fallout contamination. Housing and shelter would become unavailable for tens or hundreds of thousands of survivors. Transportation and communication would break down to rudimentary levels if they continued at all. And serious food shortages would be inevitable.

Assuming that the combatant states were to enter into nuclear conflict as modern industrial economies, these networks of highly interlocking and interdependent exchange systems would now be shattered. Virtually everyone would be deprived of his or her basic means of livelihood. Emergency police and fire services would be decimated and stressed to thoroughly ineffectual levels. All systems dependent upon electrical power would cease to function. Severe trauma would occasion widespread disorientation and psychological disorders for which there would be no therapeutic services.

Normal society, in short, would cease to function. The pestilence of unrestrained murder and banditry would augment the pestilence of plague and epidemics. With the passage of time, many of the survivors could expect an increased incidence of degenerative diseases and various kinds of cancer. They might also expect premature death, impairment of vision, and an increased likelihood of sterility. Among the survivors of Hiroshima, for example, an increased incidence of leukemia and cancer of the lung, stomach, breast, ovary, and uterine cervix has been noted.

Such a war could also have devastating climatic effects. It is now widely understood that even the explosion of a mere 100 megatons (less than 1 percent of the world's arsenals) would be enough to generate an epoch of cold and dark nearly as severe as in the 5,000-megaton case. As we have learned from Carl Sagan, the threshold for the Nuclear Winter is very low.[12]

Certain of the biological and ecological effects of a nuclear war between two countries would also be felt in other countries. Radioactive fallout does not respect political boundaries. As yields exceed 30 kilotons, part of the cloud of radioactive debris would "punch" into the stratosphere, affecting many noncombatant states.[13] If, for example, a two-country nuclear war took place in the northern hemisphere, the heating of vast quantities of dust and soot would transport these fine particles toward and across the Equator. It follows that there is little hope of reassurance for people in the northern hemisphere who feel that safety can be purchased for the price of an airline ticket to New Zealand.

Nuclear Attack by a Nuclear Weapons State against a Nonnuclear State

The spread of nuclear weapons could lead to situations wherein one rival state would possess nuclear weapons, and another might not. The combined effect of such new inequalities in international power would be a greatly increased probability of nuclear attacks against nonnuclear weapons countries. Should such attacks be carried out, what would be the expected consequences?

In terms of types of casualties and devastation, these consequences would, in all likelihood, parallel those already described in connection with two-country nuclear war. However, the actual scale and magnitude of injuries, fatalities, and physical destruction would probably be significantly smaller, since a nuclear strike against a nonnuclear country would almost surely be relatively limited in yield and counterforce in nature. It follows that as long as the purpose of the nuclear attack is a preemptive one, intended to destroy the victim side's future potential for striking first itself, something less than the total decimation of normal society could be expected.

Nevertheless, in spite of this relatively sanguine expectation, it is conceivable that the preemptive motive would be overshadowed by attitudes of national or ethnic hatred and personal bitterness. Here, rationality might give way to feelings of vengefulness, and the destructiveness of the nuclear strike could exceed levels needed for "rational" preemption. In such cases gratuitous devastation might be meted out that comes close to, or even equals, the devastation associated with a full strategic exchange between two countries.

Nuclear War between Several New Nuclear Powers

If the proliferation of nuclear weapons should lead to a nuclear war involving several new members of the nuclear club, the effects would most likely be more severe than those associated with a two-country nuclear war, but less severe than those created by nuclear war between the superpowers. Blast damage from the nuclear bursts would be enormous and extensive. Radiation would produce wide areas of radiation sickness, horrible skin burns, and huge fires.

The actual extent of these effects, of course, would depend upon the degree to which the full nuclear inventories of the combatant countries were involved. At a minimum, however, colossal destruction would be suffered in all of the target areas, and the biological/ecological after-effects would almost certainly be global. Fallout hazards, which depend on such factors as weapon design, explosive force, altitude and latitude of detonation, time of year, and local weather conditions, would descend upon both local and worldwide populations.

For example, a single nuclear weapon with a fission yield of one megaton, exploded at ground level in a 15 miles-per-hour wind, would produce fallout in an ellipse extending hundreds of miles downwind from the burst point. At a distance of 20–25 miles downwind, a lethal radiation dose would be accumulated by persons who did not find shelter within 25 minutes of the initial fallout. At a distance of 40–45 miles, persons would have no more than 3 hours after the initial fallout to find shelter. Immediately downwind of the burst point, therefore, persons who could not be sheltered or evacuated would have slim prospects for survival.[14]

If a nuclear war between several secondary nuclear powers involved the use on population centers in each country of 100 weapons of 1-megaton fission yield, more than 20 percent of each country's population would be killed immediately through blast, heat, ground shock, and instant radiation effects. A war involving 1,000 such weapons in each combatant country would destroy immediately more than half of the affected populations. And these figures do not include deaths due to fires, lack of proper medical care, starvation, or lethal fallout downwind of the burst points.[15]

Left unchecked, the proliferation of nuclear weapons threatens to bring us face to face with the torments of Dante's *Inferno,* "Into the eternal darkness, into fire, into ice." We must, therefore, begin to take measures to halt this encroachment of unbearable circumstances. More than anything else, this means a far-reaching rejection of realpolitik and its associated tolerance of an expanding nuclear club.

The time has come to challenge the strategic mythmakers on their unfounded pretensions to expertise and their intimacies with the banal syntax of power politics. Despite the apparent reasonableness of their argumentation, these nuclear mandarins speak only the language of death. Proud of their ethical illiteracy, because its suggests cold and considered calculations, they are in fact the champions of unreason. Intrigued by their own mendacities of language, they fail to recognize themselves as bearers not of safety, but of ruin and fatality.

There is little time left. Now, without further hesitation, citizens of the United States must acknowledge the imperative to survive. Today, without additional delay, we must confront a national leadership that knows nothing and wants to know nothing of truth.

Before this can happen, however, we must revive that original foundation of Americanism that has until now been drowned by the tides of unquestioning compliance—the willingness to disobey. Defied again and again by a government that gives currency to policy that is inimical and alien to truth, we must become prepared to demand of that government a last-minute disengagement from inconscience. In this connection we would not ask for a rejection of purposeful nuclear strategy, but of wizardry disguised as such a strategy.

As known by the founders of the American Republic, there can be no higher form of patriotism. Since the overriding purpose of government is to protect human life and other natural rights, a democratic government that abandons this purpose (a purpose codified in the Declaration of Independence) must be challenged by an aroused citizenry. Understood in terms of our government's ongoing flirtation with nuclear war, this suggests a clear-cut *obligation* to disobey.

At present, it seems widely believed that responsible citizenship requires nothing more than pliable and cheerful submission—submission to whatever carries the imprimatur of "official policy." Yet, this notion is entirely at odds with the major doctrinal premise of American democracy, namely that true patriotism requires disobedience when policy becomes destructive of the "unalienable" right to life. Rather than recoil from the notion of any form of disobedience, especially the limited challenge to realpolitik being advanced here, we must reaffirm our faith in American political institutions with a sustained and informed opposition.

Under current conditions blind obedience can serve only anguish and collapse. Indeed, even if the threat to survival were less ominous, it is clear that a healthy democracy tends to atrophy and decline as its citizens substitute submissiveness for vigilance. It follows that we will be justified on only one path, the path to freely acknowledged self-will and responsible dissent.

The effectiveness of official wizardry, and hence of unreason and anti-life, depends on the compliance of the bewitched. As noted by Karl Jaspers, "The magician can be swept off his feet by a responsive audience eager to give themselves in worship."[16] But it needn't end this way. Although the people of almost every society have followed the magicians again and again, the aura of magical efficacy does not surround the strategic wizards. Rather, they are enveloped by a visible cloak of deception and thoughtlessness, a vestment that makes survival possible.

Notes

1. Nuclear proliferation refers not only to the actual production of nuclear weapons by states not yet members of the nuclear club, but also to the further spread of the capability to make nuclear weapons. Since a very close relationship exists between civilian nuclear power programs and the capacity to develop nuclear weapons (such programs may provide access to weapons-usable materials, facilities, and expertise), the spread of these programs is an integral part of the proliferation problem. A state, of course, might also seek entry into the nuclear club with a research reactor to make weapons-grade plutonium or through the enrichment of uranium 235 to weapons-grade levels. In comparison to the plutonium that is made from power reactors, the plutonium from research reactors is cheaper, faster, and of higher weapons-making quality. For information on the relevance of civilian nuclear power programs to proliferation of nuclear weapons, see especially Albert Wohlstetter et al., *Swords from Plowshares: The Military Potential of Civilian Nuclear Energy* (Chicago: The University of Chicago Press, 1979); and *Nuclear Proliferation and Civilian Nuclear Power,* 9 vols., A Report of the Nonproliferation Alternative Systems Assessment Program, U.S. Department of Energy, Washington, D.C., December 1979, DOE/NE-0001, 153 pp.

2. Cited in John Herz, *International Politics in the Atomic Age* (New York: Columbia University Press, 1959), p. 212.

3. See Pierre M. Gallois, "Nuclear Strategy: A French View," in David Brook, ed., *Search for Peace* (New York: Dodd, Mead, 1970), p. 165.

4. See "Israeli Attack on Iraqi Nuclear Facilities," Hearings before the Subcommittee on International Security and Scientific Affairs on Europe and the Middle East and on International Economic Policy and Trade of the Committee on Foreign Affairs, House of Representatives, 97th Cong., 1st sess., June 17 and 25, 1981, U.S. Government Printing Office, Washington, D.C., 1981.

5. See Richard Halloran, "Spread of Nuclear Arms Is Seen by 2000," *The New York Times,* Monday, November 15, 1982, p. 3.

6. See Thomas Merton, *The Nonviolent Alternative,* Gordon C. Zahn, ed., (New York: Farrar, Straus, Giroux, 1980), p. 62.

7. See Phil Shabecoff, "Grimmer View Painted of Nuclear War Effects," *The New York Times,* Monday, October 31, 1983, p. 12.

8. Ibid.

9. See Tom Stonier, *Nuclear Disaster* (New York: Meridian, 1964), p. 24.

10. See National Academy of Sciences, *Long-Term Worldwide Effects of Multiple Nuclear Weapons Detonations,* Washington, D.C., 1975.

11. See Robert J. Lifton and E. Olson, *Living and Dying* (New York: Praeger, 1974), ch. 6.

12. See Carl Sagan, "The Nuclear Winter," A special report, *Parade Magazine,* October 30, 1983, pp. 3–7.

13. See *Worldwide Effects of Nuclear War . . . Some Perspectives,* A report of the U.S. Arms Control and Disarmament Agency, Washington, D.C., n.d., p. 7.

14. Ibid., p. 14.

15. Ibid., pp. 14–15.

16. See Karl Jaspers, *Reason and Anti-Reason in our Time,* translated by Stanley Godman (Hamden, Conn.: Archon Books, 1971), p. 74.

5 U.S. Foreign Policy on Human Rights: Discarding Dignity

The submission of the United States to realpolitik has been particularly evident in the matter of human rights. Although the Carter administration signaled a willingness to reduce such submission, this country's policy since then has been formed entirely from the perspective of the cold war. Within this perspective, it has been willing to tolerate virtually any breach of essential human dignity among its allies, who are nourished by the bile of cooperative anti-Sovietism.

Although U.S. support for authoritarian regimes is certainly not new, current policies are fraught with irony. This is the case because they flow from a tradition of persistent failure and because they seek to reverse the Carter administration's self-conscious attempt at change. Hence, these policies are both purposeless and retrograde.

As a stunning rebuke to our nation's long-standing commitment to "unalienable rights," these policies also turn aside our high ideals as if they were merely vaporous fairytales, suitable for transmittal to school children but not for the design of pragmatic international behavior.

Finally, these policies represent a stark renunciation of modern international law. While it is under no binding obligation to display moral sensitivity toward other states, the United States is bound by the peremptory norms of the law of nations, rules that endow all human beings with a basic measure of self-worth and that permit no derogation by states.

The American Political Tradition

The United States has always been committed to the idea of a higher law. Codified in both the Declaration of Independence and the Constitution, this idea is based upon the acceptance of certain principles of right and justice that prevail because of their own intrinsic merit. Eternal and immutable, they are external to all acts of human will and interpenetrate all human reason.

This idea runs continuously from the Mosaic code and the ancient Greeks[1] to the American revolution of 1776. While the entire Torah does not purport to bind humankind as a whole, a portion of it does display such intent. This view was shared by early Christian authorities, who felt that a part of Mosaic law is clearly universal, and that this part is necessarily written in the hearts of all people. Jewish and Christian thought, therefore, have long been in substantial agreement on the existence of a set of rules or precepts of conduct that is universally binding and ascertainable by human reason.

This area of agreement also has other roots. A century before Demosthenes elucidated the idea of true law as an act of *discovery,* Sophocles challenged the superiority of human rule-making in *Antigone.* Composed in 442 B.C., *Antigone* explores the basic conflict between the claims of the state and the claims of individual conscience. Antigone's appeal against King Creon's edict to the "unwritten and steadfast customs of the Gods" has since been taken to represent the incontestable supremacy of a higher law over man-made law.

Plato, disturbed by the Sophist failure to maintain a link between justice and law, sought to elevate "nature" from the sphere of contingent facts to the realm of supreme and absolute values, the realm of immutable archetypes or *Forms.* Natural law thus became the unchanging Idea of Law, which must always be the proper measure of positive law.

Aristotle later advised advocates in his *Rhetoric* that when they had no case "according to the law of the land," they should appeal "to the law of nature." Quoting the *Antigone* of Sophocles, he argued that "an unjust law is not a law." This position, of course, is in contrast to the opinion of the Sophists that justice is never more than an expression of supremacy, an opinion long since associated with the statement of Thrasymachus in Plato's *Republic:* "Right is the interest of the stronger."

Aristotle advanced the concept of "natural justice" in the *Ethics:* "Of political justice," he wrote, "part is natural, part legal—natural, that which everywhere has the same force and does not exist by people's thinking this or that; legal, that which is originally indifferent . . ." The essential ingredient of justice, then, cannot be of the state's own contrivance. It is a discovery from nature and a transcript of its constancy.[2] Its applicability, therefore, is timeless. "Not of today or yesterday its force," says Antigone, "It springs eternal: no man knows its birth."

The Stoics regarded Nature itself as the supreme legislator in a moral order where man, through his divinely granted capacity to reason, can commune directly with the gods. As set forth in *De Republica* and *De Legibus,* Cicero's concept of natural law underscores a principle that is very much a part of the American constitutional foundation: the imperative quality of the civil law is always contingent on its being in harmony with reason. According to Cicero, justice is not, as the Epicureans claimed, a matter of mere utility or the arbitrary construction of opinion. Rather, it is an institution of nature that transcends expediency and that must be embodied by positive law before such normative obligations can claim the allegiance of the human conscience.

But what is to be done when written or positive law is at variance with true law? The Romans, who cherished the idea of true law as distinct from the positive law of the state, had a remedy. They incorporated in their statutes a contingency clause that a particular law could not abrogate what was sacrosanct or *jus*. On many occasions Cicero and others invoked *jus* against one statute or another. In this way the *lex scripta,* always no more than an artifact of the civic community, remained subject to the test of conformance with nature.

The Roman concept of a higher law was widely integrated into medieval jurisprudential thought. According to John of Salisbury's *Policraticus,* "There are certain precepts of the law which have perpetual necessity, having the force of law among all nations and which absolutely cannot be broken." Recognizing the idea that all political authority must be intrinsically limited, John noted that the prince "may not lawfully have any will of his own apart from that which the law or equity enjoins, or the calculation of the common interest requires." Natural law, therefore, exists to frustrate political injustice.

Expanding upon the ancient theme of the dignity of man (the theme appears in Genesis, pervades the Old Testament, and was reinforced by early Christian emphasis on the salvation of mankind and the incarnation of Christ), Renaissance philosophers underscored the universality and centrality of human rights. However, it was left to Pico's *Oration on the Dignity of Man* to introduce a new element—man's liberty or free choice. Going beyond Giannozzo Manetti's treatise, *On the Excellency and Dignity of Man* and Ficino's *Theologia Platonica,* Pico recognizes not only man's uniqueness, but the basis of this uniqueness, which is *freedom*.

During the seventeenth and eighteenth centuries, natural law doctrine was reaffirmed and strengthened by Grotius and Newton. Reviving the Ciceronian idea of natural law and its underlying optimism about human nature, Grotius must be credited with freeing this idea from any dependence on ecclesiastical or papal interpretation. Newton's English deism provided scholars with the foundations for entire systems from which judicial rights and obligations could be deduced with Euclidean precision.

The actual conveyance of natural law thinking into American constitutional theory—a conveyance that is largely responsible for the irony of current American foreign policy on human rights—was the work of John Locke's *Second Treatise on Civil Government.* While Hobbes regarded natural law and civil law as coextensive, Locke echoed a more than two thousand year tradition with his view that the validity of civil law must always be tested against antecedent natural law. The codified American duty to revolt when governments commit "a long train of abuses and usurpations" flows from Locke's notion that civil authority can never extend beyond the securing of man's natural rights.

Moreover, the Declaration of Independence codified a social contract that sets limits on the power of *any* government. Its purpose was to define a set of *universally valid* constraints upon secular political authority. Since justice, which is based on natural law, binds all human society, the rights articulated by the Declaration of Independence cannot be reserved only to Americans. Rather, they must extend to all human societies and can never be contravened by positive or written law.

This theory of natural law, which had been fully secularized by Pufendorf and Vattel as well as by Grotius, is based on clarity, self-evidence, and coherence. Its validity cannot be shaken by the reality of bad governments. And its preeminent emphasis on the value and dignity of each individual is not subject to revision by civil law. It follows that the principles of our own Declaration of Independence must shape not only our own domestic political relations, but our relations with other peoples as well. To do otherwise would be illogical and self-contradictory, since it would nullify the immutable and universal law of nature from which the Declaration derives.

Yet the ethics of humanitarianism, which have had a particular resonance in the American tradition, are today no longer a beacon to an unregenerate world. In the fashion of Sophocles' Creon, who is transformed from a sympathetic figure in *Oedipus the King* to a decidedly unsympathetic one in the *Antigone,* the United States has evolved from a position of championing human rights to one of reflexively and selectively opposing them. Although this evolution has been taking place since the eighteenth century, the fullest rejection of its own traditions has—with the brief and partial exception of the Carter administration—been forged in the realpolitik dynamic of the cold war. Resting its position on a series of assumptions that is much closer to the Christian doctrine of original sin than to the Ciceronian idea of human dignity, the Reagan administration has now completed the severance of American foreign policy from American political tradition.

This severance, of course, is not intended to support or produce evil. Rather, it recognizes evil as an unwanted but unavoidable by-product of policy in an imperfect world. Since it accepts Machiavelli's instruction from Chapter XV of *The Prince,* "A man who wishes to make a profession of goodness in everything must necessarily come to grief among so many who are not good," the administration also accepts the dilemma of practicing goodness in an essentially wicked world. More recently, this dilemma has been expressed by Reinhold Niebuhr's idea of the tragic aspect of contemporary history:

> The tragic element in a human situation is constituted of conscious choices of evil for the sake of good. If men or nations do evil in a good cause; if

> they cover themselves with guilt in order to fulfill some high responsibility; or if they sacrifice some high value for the sake of a higher or equal one they make a tragic choice.[3]

But Niebuhr's imperative is markedly self-contradictory, offering a perennial pretext for those people who prefer evil and an irresistible incentive to those who prefer to believe that evil cannot be avoided. In the fashion of Jean-Paul Sartre's portrait of the anti-Semite in *Anti-Semite and Jew,* such people always choose evil with "pure heart." Since they do evil "for the sake of good," they inevitably look upon themselves as *sanctified* evildoers. Hence, though they may censure their most murderous instincts, they are able to accord esteem and enthusiasm to all forms of violence with an altogether clear conscience. Fully accepting their accommodation with evil, they feel in themselves the lightness of heart and peace of mind that accompany the satisfaction of a job well done, of a duty properly discharged.

In this connection Hannah Arendt's concept of the "banality of evil," nurtured by her attendance at the Eichmann trial in Jerusalem, is also pertinent to our understanding of the issues. Evil, Arendt teaches us, is not always something that is self-consciously demonic. Indeed, monstrous deeds are often done by "ordinary" individuals who are manifestly shallow. The impetus for these deeds comes from thoughtlessness.

In its current foreign policy concerning human rights, the United States displays the same kind of thoughtlessness that it displays in its nuclear strategy. The wickedness of this policy is occasioned not by depravity or base motives, but by the literal incapacity to reason. Before this policy can be reversed, our leaders will have to abandon their models of circular sophistry in favor of more acceptable patterns of knowing, patterns that reflect the essential convergence of normative and analytic investigations.[4]

The United States now lives outside history, in parentheses. Ever fearful of metamorphoses that represent its only hope for survival, it can no longer abide the seductive virulence of a realpolitik orientation to human rights. Accepting the Latin maxim *jus ex injuria non oritur* (rights do not arise from wrongs), it must grasp the immutable principles of its own traditions, acknowledging them as the only proper and pragmatic standard for further global interactions.

"When I get to heaven," said the Hasidic Rabbi Susya just before his death, "they will not ask me, 'Why were you not Moses?' but 'Why were you not Susya?' " When the United States confronts the consequences of its current "geopolitical" strategy, its people will not ask, "Why were we not saints?" but "Why were we not Americans?" Why did we not become what we could become? Why did we act in a manner contrary to our own unique potentiality? Why did we abandon our traditions and our interests at the same time?

The Jurisprudential Imperative

The retreat of the United States from human rights in foreign affairs is more than an ironic break with its own revolutionary traditions. It is also a rejection of certain peremptory norms (*jus cogens*) of international law. While the break with tradition falls within the volitional ambit of states in world politics, the rejection of incontrovertible juridical standards does not. Rather, such rejection represents a breach of internationally accepted rules and principles of action that endangers the entire edifice of civilized international relations. Such an understanding is already built into the State Department's annual *Country Reports on Human Rights Practices.* According to the Introduction to this Report:

> There now exists an international consensus that recognizes basic human rights and obligations owed by all governments to their citizens. This consensus is reflected in a growing body of international law: the Universal Declaration of Human Rights; the International Covenant on Economic, Social and Cultural Rights; and other international and regional human rights agreements. . . . These internationally-recognized rights can be grouped into three broad categories:
>
> —first, the right to be free from governmental violations of the integrity of the person—violations such as torture, cruel, inhuman or degrading treatment or punishment; arbitrary arrest or imprisonment; denial of fair public trial; and invasion of the home.
>
> —second, the right to the fulfillment of vital needs such as food, shelter, health care and education;
>
> —third, the right to enjoy civil and political liberties, including freedom of speech, press, religion and assembly; the right to participate in government; the right to travel freely within and outside one's own country; the right to be free from discrimination based on race or sex.[5]

Since the end of the Second World War, there has been a revolution in international legal affairs. Among other things this revolution has removed a state's treatment of its own nationals from the realm of "domestic jurisdiction" whenever such treatment fails to conform to particular normative standards. Expanding upon the long-standing principle of humanitarian intervention, the Nuremberg judgment and Nuremberg Principles place additional and far-reaching limits on the authority of particular states. Reasoning that the individual human being, as the ultimate unit of all law, is entitled to the protection of humankind when the state tramples upon its rights, the Tribunal firmly established the *obligation* of states to intervene in other states whenever grievous outrages are committed.[6]

In the absence of viable community enforcement capabilities in our decentralized international society, the opportunities for justice require voluntary patterns of compliance and support by individual governments. The prevailing expectation is that such patterns will be especially acknowledged by the world's major powers. It follows that punishment of gross violations of human rights is now well within the jurisdictional scope of American foreign policy.

If the United States continues to turn its back on responsible enforcement of the international law of human rights, it will lose not only its few remaining claims to moral leadership, but also its last practical chance for harmony with the developing world. Indeed, our retrograde policy on human rights may soon lose this country its friends as well. The problem lies in recognizing the principle of "just cause" for insurgency (a principle enshrined in our traditions and in the law of nations) and in distinguishing between lawful and unlawful insurgencies under international law.

The American imperative must be to condemn not only insurgent terror, but also "regime" terror. Regime terror, which contradicts the extant rules and principles of international law, *breeds* insurgent terror. If the United States is to be true to the basic ideals of its founding documents as well as to its international legal obligations and long-term geopolitical interests, it cannot continue to support the former while combating the latter. In this connection our leaders might take another look at the annual State Department Report, *Country Reports on Human Rights Practices,* a report that regularly identifies a large number of countries that engage in the systematic and unlawful denial of essential human rights to their citizens.

Today many of these countries are told that such denial will be tolerated by the United States so long as there is consistent support for cooperative anti-Sovietism. Founded upon a spurious dichotomy between authoritarian and totalitarian regimes, this policy stipulates that monstrous violations of human dignity from the political right are acceptable, but that from the left they are not. This myopic policy will inevitably fail as the oligarchs are eclipsed and their successors join the expanding legion of anti-American states.

To prevent such failure, the United States need only begin to adhere to its own national legal and doctrinal obligations. The basic principles of the international law of human rights have already been incorporated into the laws of the United States. The Department of State is obligated to enforce the human rights provisions mandated by sections 116(d) and 502B(b) of the Foreign Assistance Act of 1961 as amended.[7] Although it is true that security assistance may be provided to human rights violators if "extraordinary circumstances exist which necessitate a continuance of security assistance," an overzealous discovery of such circumstances would have the effect of subverting both national and international law. This point was understood by former Secretary of State Cyrus Vance, who offered the following observation to the Senate Committee on Foreign Relations on March 27, 1980: "We pursue our human rights objectives, not only because they are right, but because we have a stake in the stability that comes when people can express their hopes and find their futures freely. Our ideals and our interests coincide."

Who are the terrorists? Are they the black South African guerrillas who oppose a white minority-ruled apartheid regime? Are they the individuals among the neighboring frontline states—Angola, Botswana, Zambia, Zimbabwe, Mozambique, and Tanzania—who support black South African insurgents? Are they the Namibians who support the South-West African People's Organization (SWAPO) in a U.N.-sanctioned opposition to South African control? Are they the Salvadoran guerrillas who confront *las catorce familias* (the 14 families) to escape from grinding poverty? Are they also the rightist death squads that operate throughout Latin America? What about the Afghan Muslim guerrillas combating Soviet troops or Iran's ethnic Kurds, who have taken up arms on the side of Iraq? And what about the Cuban and Nicaraguan exiles who continue to operate with official U.S. support?

The problem, of course, is exceedingly complex. During the coming months and years, the United States will have to make very critical distinctions between terrorists and legitimate revolutionary movements. And these distinctions will have to be based on more important criteria than shortsighted definitions of self-interest. Even in narrow geopolitical terms, a continuing American retreat from human rights in foreign affairs will ultimately have devastating repercussions. In South Africa, for example, the winds of change are clear and unstoppable. At some point in the not-too-distant future, our access to that country's vital mineral resources will depend upon our commitment to black majority rule.

What features of the international legal order underscore the principle of "just cause?" Although world law has consistently condemned particular acts of international terrorism, it has also countenanced certain uses of force that derive from "the inalienable right to self-determination and independence of all peoples under colonial and racist regimes and other forms of alien domination and the legitimacy of their struggle, in particular the struggle of national liberation movements, in accordance with the purposes and principles of the Charter and the relevant resolutions of the organs of the United Nations." This exemption, from the 1973 General Assembly Report of the Ad Hoc Committee on International Terrorism, is corroborated—of course—by Article 7 of the U.N. General Assembly's 1974 Definition of Aggression: "Nothing in this definition, and in particular Article 3 [inventory of acts that qualify as aggression] could in any way prejudice the right to self-determination, freedom, and independence, as derived from the Charter, of peoples forcibly deprived of that right and referred to in the Declaration of Principles of International Law concerning Friendly Relations and Cooperation among States in accordance with the Charter of the United Nations particularly peoples under colonial and racist regimes or other forms of alien domination; nor the right of these peoples to struggle to that end and to seek and receive support, in accordance with the principles of the Charter and in conformity with the above-mentioned Declaration."

International law, therefore, actually supports the legitimacy of certain forms of insurgency. While this is important in light of the objectives of international justice, it does create severe problems in promoting the objectives of international order. The ultimate problem, of course, is allowing international law to serve the interests of order without impairing the legitimate interests of justice.

But how are we to determine the proper balance? And what criteria can be applied? Given the structure of a decentralized system of international law, individual states must bear the final responsibility for distinguishing between terrorism and lawful acts of insurgency.

What principles should inform their judgments? First, careful assessments must be made of particular regimes' conformance with the international law of human rights. Regime terror spawns revolutionary violence and must be opposed strenuously by the community of nations.

Second, states must exhibit a deep and abiding concern for discrimination and proportionality in evaluating the legitimacy of insurgent uses of force. Once force is applied to any segment of human population, blurring the distinction between combatants and noncombatants, terrorism has surfaced. Similarly, once force is applied to the fullest possible extent, restrained only by the limits of available weaponry, terrorism is taking place.

In the words of the Report of the General Assembly's Ad Hoc Committee on International Terrorism (1973): "Even when the use of force is legally and morally justified, there are some means, as in every form of human conflict, which must not be used; the legitimacy of a cause does not in itself legitimize the use of certain forms of violence, especially against the innocent." As in the case of war between states, every use of force by insurgents must be judged twice; once with regard to the justness of the objective, and once with regard to the justness of the means used in the fighting.

There is, however, a reciprocal obligation of states to treat captured insurgents in conformity with the basic dictates of humanity. While this obligation does not normally interfere with a state's right to regard as common or ordinary criminals those persons not engaged in armed conflict (persons involved in internal disturbances, riots, isolated and specific acts of violence, or other acts of similar nature), it does mean that all captives (according to the Geneva Conventions of August 1949) "remain under the protection and authority of the principles of international law derived from established custom, from the principles of humanity and from the dictates of public conscience." In cases where captive persons *are* engaged in armed conflict, it means an additional obligation of states to extend the privileged status of prisoner of war to such persons. Moreover, this additional obligation is unaffected by insurgent respect for the laws of war. While all combatants are obliged to comply with the rules of international law applicable in armed conflict, violations of these rules do not deprive an insurgent combatant of his right to protection equivalent in all respects to those accorded to prisoners of war.

This right, codified by the Geneva Conventions of August 1949, is now complemented and enlarged by two protocols to those conventions.

Protocol I makes the law concerning international conflicts applicable to conflicts fought for self-determination against alien occupation and against colonialist and racist regimes. A product of the Diplomatic Conference on the Reaffirmation and Development of International Humanitarian Law Applicable in Armed Conflicts that ended on June 10, 1977, Protocol I (which was justified by the decolonization provisions of the UN Charter and by resolutions of the General Assembly) bring irregular forces within the full scope of the law of armed conflict.[8]

Protocol II, also additional to the Geneva Conventions of August 12, 1949, concerns protection of victims of noninternational armed conflicts. Hence, this Protocol applies to all armed conflicts not covered by Protocol I and that take place within the territory of a state between its armed forces and dissident armed forces. These dissident armed forces, to be under the ambit of Protocol II and therefore of international law, must be "under responsible command" and must "exercise such control over a part of its territory as to enable them to carry out sustained and concerted military operations and to implement this Protocol."

In the aftermath of the Holocaust, the philosopher Karl Jaspers addressed himself to the question of German guilt. His response to this question articulates one of the most fertile and important concepts of modern thought, the idea of "metaphysical guilt." In this connection, wrote Jaspers: "There exists a solidarity among men as human beings that makes each co-responsible for every wrong and every injustice in the world, especially for crimes committed in his presence or with his knowledge. If I fail to do whatever I can to prevent them, I too am guilty." Understood in terms of this country's current unconcern for ongoing crimes against humanity, Jaspers' doctrine suggests an urgent need to confront overriding Nuremberg obligations, a need that challenges us both individually and collectively to oppose such crimes while there is still time.

From the point of view of the United States, the Nuremberg obligations are, in a sense, doubly binding. This is the case because these obligations represent not only current normative obligations of international law, but also the doctrinal obligations engendered by the American political tradition. By its codification of the principle that fundamental human rights are not an internal question for each state, but an imperious postulate of the international community, the Nuremberg obligations represent a point of perfect convergence between the law of nations and the jurisprudential/ethical foundations of the American republic.

Nuremberg established, beyond any reasonable doubt, the continuing validity of natural law argumentations. While the indictments of the Nuremberg Tribunal were cast in terms of existing or positive international law, the actual decisions of the tribunal unambiguously reject the proposition that the validity of law depends upon its "positiveness." The words used by the tribunal ("So far from it being unjust to punish him, it would be unjust if his wrongs were allowed to go unpunished") derive from the principle *nullum crimen sine poena* (no crime without a punishment). This principle is a flat contradiction of the extreme position of positive jurisprudence, which ties punishment to a very narrow definition of man-made law.

As an answer to the question, *quid ius?*—"What is law?"—international law now rejects all empirical solutions that substitute force for justice. Rather than accept the neo-Kantian distinction between the "concept" and the "ideal" of law, international law now recognizes that the concept and the ideal coincide. The law of nations, like all laws, is therefore a branch of ethics. Taken together with the understanding that the supremacy of natural law has always been part of the American tradition, and that the current position of international law includes an "incorporation" of this tradition, this conclusion suggests an overriding need for change in America's foreign policy on human rights.

Toward a New U.S. Foreign Policy on Human Rights

The birth of an improved American foreign policy on human rights will have to be fashioned incrementally. How can this happen? Clearly, the ethical, traditional, and legal imperatives already discussed are an insufficient basis for transforming American foreign policy. To expect these imperatives to have an independent effect would be to commit the worst fallacies of utopianism. Before the United States can turn from its current direction on human rights, its leaders will have to calculate that such a turn would be in our own national interests. The task, then, is to discover areas of convergence between the aforementioned imperatives and perceived strategies of self-interest. This country will turn to a lawful policy on human rights only when it understands that by supporting the punishment of crimes against humanity it protects not only the interests of the international community, but its own interests as well.

What can foster such understanding? To begin, a growing number of people throughout the world are already distressed by the inhumane values of U.S. foreign policy. Many Americans are concerned that we must accept complicity in the retrograde actions of our government and that we may therefore lose any claims to bear witness as a truly righteous people.

The U.S. policy on human rights perpetuates the image of America as oppressor. While the American revolutionary tradition views natural law as a goal toward which positive law inevitably tends, this policy regards natural law as a standard from which human authority inevitably strays. Consequently, both our ideals and our normative obligations are now self-consciously subordinated to the presumed requirements of expediency.

In the final analysis, however, these requirements will surely prove illusory, since the subordination of ethical and legal obligations will be widely imitated by other states. The results of this American policy, then, will be increasing worldwide *instability.* By acting on the assumptions of realpolitik, the United States will inevitably contribute to a continuation of the Darwinian dynamics of the *bellum omnes contra omnes* (war of all against all) in international society. The prophecy will be self-fulfilled.

The nations in world politics coexist in a perilously fragile network of relationships that can no longer abide the conflictual dynamics of structural inequality. Unless the United States begins to recognize that its own interests must be defined from the standpoint of what is just for the system as a whole, these interests will not be sustained. Rather, they will crumble along with the rest of a foreign policy edifice that is collapsing under the weight of its own insensitivity.

Founded upon a fear of both past and future, the Reagan administration's central thrust toward counterrevolutionary intervention has generated a terrifying kind of aloneness—an isolation in time—that is best characterized by the existential credo: "To live now is all there is, over and over and over again." This idea has less in common with the Nietzschean doctrine of the eternal recurrence of the same events than it does with Spengler's notion of time as the very meaning of the historical world-picture, as an "inner certainty," as "destiny itself." Approached in terms of this notion, America's current worldview suggests a static and unchanging orientation to global affairs that is inherently self-defeating.

To a certain extent this orientation mirrors the quintessential errors of Western culture: unrestrained egotism, excessive elitism, and social-Darwinism. It is almost a Faustian dilemma: How can true fulfillment abide the presence of unbridled self-centeredness? For the United States and for the rest of the world, survival requires a renunciation of the principle, "Everyone for himself." It is no longer possible to cite as "realistic" a foreign policy of national advantage that is at cross-purpose with the spirit of worldwide dignity and well-being. It is time to replace the impersonal logic of possessive individualism in world politics with the organic morality of mutual regard and concern.

In its basic distinction between totalitarian and authoritarian regimes, the U.S. clarifies that what it finds objectionable is not the violation of human rights within states, but the enlargement of military power by our adversaries. In the words of former Secretary of State Haig's speech to the Trilateral Commission in Washington on March 31, 1981: "We should distinguish between the deprivation of national rights through aggression and the deprivation of personal rights through oppression." Since this distinction parallels the "difference" between totalitarian and authoritarian regimes, our real concern, said Haig, must be with the former: "The totalitarian regimes tend to be intolerable at home and abroad, actively hostile to all we represent and ideologically resistant to political change." It goes without saying, however, that this distinction has no basis in our own traditions or in international law. This spurious distinction serves to undermine any remaining hopes for a world public order of human dignity.

In making anti-Sovietism the centerpiece of its policy on human rights, the U.S. effectively accepts the pernicious doctrine that there is no law but positive law, that might equals right. Confronting a world where Kafka's fiction of arbitrary arraignment and punishment has already become a widely institutionalized historical fact, the U.S. indicates that it will "not take sides" between blacks and whites in South Africa. As in the Melian Dialogues of Thucydides, which relate the negotiations between the Athenians and the Melians during the Peloponnesian War, the standard of justice applied by the United States "depends on the equality of power to compel." In such a world, one where "the strong do what they have power to do and the weak accept what they have to accept," the United States endorses an inscrutably perverse logic by which support for Nazi-type regimes is reconciled with what the Reagan administration once called "our nation's self-expression."

Our government claims that it is pursuing a more effective means of support for human rights: silent diplomacy. In this connection one must heed the words of Jacobo Timerman: "Silent diplomacy is silence, and quiet diplomacy is surrender."[9] During the coming months and years, the United States must begin to act upon the wisdom of Martin Buber's philosophy of dialogue, substituting the openness, directness, and mutuality of the "I–Thou" relationship for the subject–object relationship of the "I–It." Entangled in vainglorious delusions of power and responsibility, this nation can no longer abide a relationship with peoples in other states that knows and uses them apart from their own uniqueness. To supplant the procrustean relations cultivated by current American foreign policy, the United States must learn to experience the other side of its relations. Through such an act of "inclusion," as Buber calls it, this country can extend its knowledge of others to a point where respect for human rights flows naturally between partners in a "dialogue."

The mark of contemporary man is that he does not really listen. Yet only when one really listens can there be a meeting with others and a progression to the sphere of the "between" that Buber knows to be the "really real." Understood in terms of America's now institutionalized unconcern for human rights, this suggests a need to listen to the needs of individuals everywhere. The resultant dialogue and communication would be of service not only to these other individuals, but also to the self of this nation through authentic feelings of relatedness.

An example of America's failure to listen is President Reagan's participation at the Cancun talks in October 1981. Confronted by developing nations of the southern hemisphere that are heavily burdened by energy costs and mounting debt, Mr. Reagan called on those nations to develop free market economies that would permit a greater flow of private investment and trade. In other words, said the president, the only reasonable countermeasure to abject poverty is "the American way."

What Mr. Reagan ignored, however, is that the world economy is rigged against the developing countries. As producers of raw materials, they sell their wares in largely competitive markets but buy finished goods from a handful of producers who are unencumbered by competition. Receiving less and less while paying more and more, the developing countries are perennially disadvantaged. Julius Nyerere, president of Tanzania and a Cancun participant, captured the essence of these declining terms of trade with his remark that "poor countries almost always buy dear and sell cheap." To change this situation, these countries have demanded a shift in power relations and a "massive transfer of resources" from the rich to the poor.

But the president of the United States refused to listen. Rather than recognize the stated differences between north and south, he insisted with unusual vehemence that the key to development lies in private investment. And he made this argument in spite of the fact that the essential elements of entrepreneurship and open markets are absent throughout much of the Third World.

Human becomes human with the other self. Nations become nations with the other nations. The task is to make the United States conscious of its vital planetary identity. With such a redefinition of national interest, we can progress from the dying forms of realpolitik to the primordial power of human unity and interdependence.

The primary arena of an improved world public order of human dignity is *intra*national. And the primary sector of intranational transformation is the United States. Since there exist no centralized institutions of truly authoritative character in the international legal order to identify wrongdoings, adjudicate differences, and apply punishments, ultimate responsibility for these legal functions continues to reside within the separate states. It follows that this country must take steps to ensure that, throughout the world, the authority relation between those who command and those who obey rests upon what Hannah Arendt calls "the hierarchy itself, whose rightness and legitimacy both recognize, and where both have their predetermined stable place."[10]

By taking such steps, the United States would give meaningful content to President Reagan's October 19, 1981 comments before 60,000 celebrants of the victory of Yorktown in 1781 that the battle against the British was "won by and for all who cherish the timeless and universal rights of man." Mr. Reagan's address, representing the final installment of this nation's bicentennial festivities, went on to affirm the United States as a "beacon of freedom" shining on other nations whose citizens are deprived of human rights. As we have already seen, however, the task remains to transform this beacon from histrionic oratory to serious foreign policy. Without such transformation, the president's remarks must stand only as an expression of the dead world of obligatory public pronouncements, a world where the destruction of values has reached a point where the bewildered head of the American state can no longer distinguish between appearance and reality.

By taking such steps, the president would give authentic expression to U.S. human rights policy as mandated by the congressional directive of Section 502B of the Foreign Assistance Act that "a principal goal of the foreign policy of the United States is to promote the increased observance of internationally recognized human rights." In this connection, pursuant to the accepted imperatives of the State Department's *Country Reports on Human Rights Practices,* all decisions on foreign assistance by the United States must take human rights conditions into primary account. And more particular expressions of current policy must be given more than simple obeisance. The following standards identified by the Department of State are a good place to begin:

> The transfer of police and military equipment is carefully reviewed in order to avoid identifying the United States with repressive practices. In addition, the human rights policy employs a varied mix of diplomatic tools: frank discussions with foreign officials; meetings with victims of human rights abuses; and, where private diplomacy is unavailing or unavailable, public statements of concern.[11]

At first glance, the attractiveness of increasing American support for human rights in other states appears to have been strengthened considerably by the November 1981 State Department memorandum on human rights policy. Prepared by then Deputy Secretary of State William P. Clark and Under Secretary of State for Management Richard T. Kennedy, this memorandum stipulated that, "Human rights is at the core of our foreign policy because it is central to what America is and stands for." At the same time, however, this document cast the entire issue of expanded U.S. concern for human rights within the standard geopolitical context of Soviet–American competition. Thus, the memorandum continued:

> Human rights—meaning political rights and civil liberties—conveys what is ultimately at issue in our contest with the Soviet bloc. The fundamental distinction is our respective attitudes toward freedom. Our ability to resist the Soviets around the world depends in part on our ability to draw this distinction and to persuade others of it.

As in all other elements of the Reagan administration's foreign policy, the memorandum defined "the central distinction in international politics" as a Manichean struggle "between free nations and those that are not free." And since it recognized only a single, bipolar axis of international conflict, this distinction is paralleled unambiguously by anti-Soviet and pro-Soviet states. There are no complicating or interpenetrating dimensions. The problem is clear and straightforward. It is all a question of the manner in which nonsuperpower states align themselves.

"We desire to demonstrate," continued the memorandum, "by acting to defend liberty and identifying its enemies, that the difference between East and West is the crucial political distinction of our times." With so shallow an understanding of the essential dynamics of world politics, it follows that the United States cannot be expected to support human rights indiscriminately. Rather, this country's "response or retaliatory actions should result from a balancing of all pertinent interests," which is an inoffensive way of saying that we must continue to support repressive regimes of the right in the overriding interest of cooperative anti-Sovietism.

We are, tragically, in for more of the same. "Human rights," said the memorandum, "is not advanced by replacing a bad regime with a worse one, or a corrupt dictator with a zealous Communist politburo." Unable to free itself from the dangerously limiting confines of a unidimensional world view, the Department of State continues to express its opposition to human rights violations in the simplified accents of the cold war. Unable to understand the primacy of gross structural inequalities in explaining the conditions of an endangered planet, it can only recommend a perpetual contest between the forces of light and the forces of darkness. Unable even at the rhetorical level to acknowledge the intrinsic importance of human rights, it suggests only that "A human rights policy means trouble, for it means hard choices which may adversely affect certain bilateral relations."

Gabriela Mistral, the Chilean poet who won the Nobel Prize for Literature in 1945, once wrote that crimes against humanity carry within themselves "a moral judgment over an evil in which every feeling man and woman concurs." At this time in our national history, the last real hope for preventing such evil lies in compliance with the complementary imperatives of our traditions and our legal norms. With such compliance, the United States could replace its still growing incapacity for compassionate and purposeful interaction with a timely ethos of planetary renewal.

Notes

1. The Mosaic code, of course, advanced a notion of singularity wherein all humankind are God's children, made in His image. Strictly speaking, this code had no need for a distinct concept of "natural law." Since all law proceeds from God, law is always just. At the same time, while early Jewish legal theory had no need for developing a distinction between natural and positive law, this theory had all of the essential markings of natural law. This is the case because it constrains humankind within a transcendant order revealed by divine word and interpreted by human reason.

The Greek idea of natural law probably begins with the fragments of Heraclitus (c. 500 B.C.) which reveal the following principle: "For all human laws are nourished by one, which is divine. For it governs as far as it will, and is sufficient for all, and more than enough." Such Heraclitean *dicta* entered into later Stoic philosophy and offered the vision of one universal rational law with which things "in their nature" are always in accord.

2. See Edward S. Corwin, *The Higher Law Background of American Constitutional Law* (Ithaca, N.Y.: Cornell University Press, 1929), p. 8.

3. See Reinhold Niebuhr, *The Irony of American History* (New York: Scribner's, 1952), Preface, p. vii.

4. See Hannah Arendt, *The Life of the Mind* (New York: Harcourt, Brace, Jovanovich, 1978).

5. See *Country Reports on Human Rights Practices,* Report submitted to the Committee on Foreign Relations, U.S. Senate, and Committee on Foreign Affairs, U.S. House of Representatives, by the Department of State, 97th Cong., 1st sess., February 2, 1981.

6. See especially the statement by the British Chief Prosecutor, *The Charter and Judgment of the Nuremberg Tribunal: History and Analysis,* Memorandum submitted by the Secretary-General, United Nations, General Assembly, International Law Commission, Lake Success, N.Y., 1949, p. 71.

7. The State Department reports on individual country human rights practices also fulfill the legislative requirement of Section 31 of the Bretton Woods Agreement Act.

8. Interestingly enough, the human rights conserving policy of Protocol I was prefigured by a recent American step to promote humane treatment of irregulars. During the Southeast Asia conflict, the U.S. government accorded prisoner-of-war (POW) status upon capture to irregulars under the terms of U.S. Army Military Assistance Command, Vietnam (MACV) Directive 381-46 (December 27, 1967). This directive, building upon the common Article 3 of the four Geneva Conventions of 1949, accorded POW status to irregulars who did not meet the requirements of Article 4A(2) of the Geneva POW Convention.

9. See Jacobo Timerman, *Prisoner without a Name, Cell without a Number* (New York: Knopf, 1981).

10. See Hannah Arendt, "What Was Authority?" in Carl Friedrich, ed., *Authority* (Cambridge, Mass.: Harvard University Press, 1958), p. 82.

11. See *Country Reports on Human Rights Practices;* p. 5. In this connection, we must take special note of ongoing American efforts to "destabilize" the governments of Cuba and Nicaragua. Such efforts, of course, are not only fraught with irony (in view of indignant American objections to alleged Cuban and Nicaraguan support for insurgents in El Salvador), but also *prima facie* instances of aggression under international law. This is the case because the legal systems embodied in the constitutions of particular states are part of the international legal order and are therefore an interest that all states must defend against external attack.

While, as we have already seen, this obligation is reversed by international law where the governments in question stand in marked opposition to the overriding imperatives of human rights (a reversal prefigured by Hugo Grotius in Book 2 of *The Law of War and Peace* and by Samuel Pufendorf in Book 8 of *The Law of Nature and Nations*), there is no pertinent evidence of such opposition with Cuba or Nicaragua. This is not to suggest that the revolutionary governments in these states are beyond reproach in terms of compliance with the international law of human rights, but, rather, that these governments are visibly more satisfactory than their predecessors. And American efforts to train anti-Castro exiles and former members of Somoza's National Guard for new "Mongoose" operations are hardly motivated by the search to improve human rights in Cuba and Nicaragua.

In support of the principle that foreign military intervention is unlawful unless it is understood as an indispensable corrective to gross violations of human rights, most texts and treatises on international law have long expressed the opinion (an authoritative *source* of international law according to Article 38 of the Statute of the International Court of Justice) that a state is forbidden to allow its territory to be used as a base for aggressive operations against another state with which it is not at war. Building upon the widely recognized jurisprudential foundations of Liszt and Oppenheim, Hersch Lauterpacht formulated the following peremptory norm concerning the scope of state responsibility for preventing and repressing revolutionary or counterrevolutionary acts of private persons against foreign states:

> International law imposes upon the State the duty of restraining persons within its territory from engaging in such revolutionary activities against friendly States as amount to organized acts of force in the form of hostile expeditions against the territory of those States. It also obliges the State to repress and discourage activities in which attempts against the life of political opponents are regarded as a proper means of revolutionary action." (See Hersch Lauterpacht, *International Law,* vol. 3., *The Law of Peace,* Parts 2–6 (Cambridge, England: Cambridge University Press, 1977), p. 274.

Lauterpacht's rule reaffirms the *Resolution on the Rights and Duties of Foreign Powers as Regards the Established and Recognized Governments in Case of Insurrection,* adopted by the Institute of International Law in 1900. (Section 3 of Article 2 prohibits states to allow a hostile military expedition against an established and recognized government to be organized within its territory: a prohibition now subject to modification only in the interests of humanitarian intervention). This prohibition represents a refinement of the prescription advanced by the eighteenth century Swiss scholar, Emeric de Vattel. According to Book 2 of Vattel's *The Law of Nations,* states that support insurgency against other lawful states become the legitimate prey of the community of mankind: "If there should be found a restless and unprincipled nation, ever ready to do harm to others, to thwart their purposes, and to stir up civil strife among their citizens, there is no doubt that all others would have the right to unite together to subdue such a nation, to discipline it, and even to disable it from doing further harm."

Today, the long-standing customary prohibitions against foreign support for lawless insurgencies is codified in the UN Charter and in the authoritative interpretation of that multilateral treaty in Article 1 and Article 3(g) of the 1974 UN General Assembly Definition of Aggression.

6 U.S. Foreign Policy on Human Rights: Genocide

The most pernicious abuse of human rights is genocide. Sadly, U.S. commitment to realpolitik has prevented the effective enforcement of antigenocide norms. These norms are now a clearly articulated and binding expectation of international law.

Although it has been shaped to fit a variety of political conditions for polemical purposes, genocide has a definite jurisprudential meaning. Based upon a combination of the Greek *genos* (meaning race or tribe) with the Latin *cide* (meaning killing), it means the commission of certain specific acts with particular kinds of intent. Coined in 1944 by Raphael Lemkin, a Polish lawyer who escaped the German occupation of his homeland, it describes what Winston Churchill once called "a crime without a name." In this connection it describes a crime that is juristically distinct from other sorts of wartime killing (killing long since prohibited by the laws of war of international law) and from other sorts of nonwartime political repression.

According to Articles II and III of the Genocide Convention, which entered into force on January 12, 1951:

Article II

In the present Convention, genocide means any of the following acts committed with intent to destroy, in whole or in part, a national, ethnical, racial or religious group as such:

(a) Killing members of the group;
(b) Causing serious bodily or mental harm to members of the group;
(c) Deliberately inflicting on the group conditions of life calculated to bring about its physical destruction in whole or in part;
(d) Imposing measures intended to prevent births within the group;
(e) Forcibly transferring children of the group to another group.

Article III

The following acts shall be punishable:

(a) Genocide;
(b) Conspiracy to commit genocide;
(c) Direct and public incitement to commit genocide;
(d) Attempt to commit genocide;
(e) Complicity in genocide.

Although legal scholars may understand that genocide has *always* been prohibited by international law (in the words of the Genocide Convention,

"Genocide is a modern word for an old crime") the post-World War II criminalization of genocide has been especially explicit and far-reaching. Building upon the norms established by international custom, the general principles of law recognized by civilized nations, the writings of highly qualified publicists, various treaties and conventions and the overriding principles of natural law, this criminalization has taken place under allied and UN auspicies and has flowed almost entirely from universal reaction to the Holocaust.

Prior to 1945, no principle of international law was more widely revered in practice than the idea of "domestic jurisdiction" on matters relating to human rights. On these matters, the rule of nonintervention was effectively absolute. Thus, what went on within one state's own borders was effectively no one else's affair.

In theory, of course, the idea of absolute nonintervention had already been shattered by a number of pertinent treaties and conventions before World War II. Both the Treaty of Westphalia in 1648 (ending the Thirty Years War) and the so-called Minorities Treaties after World War I did undertake to protect specific groups within states from inhuman treatment. During the period between these norm-making agreements, the Treaties of Vienna (1815) provided for abolition of the slave trade—abolition that was reinforced by provisions of the Brussels Anti-Slavery Conference (1890). And the Geneva Convention of 1864 prescribed specific patterns for the treatment of the sick and wounded in time of war. Yet no truly universal, comprehensive, and codified protection of human rights existed before 1945.

After the Second World War, the Nuremberg Tribunal was established and in session (1945–1949). Based upon its Charter (the London Charter of 1944), this specially constituted international tribunal brought charges on three categories of crime under international law: crimes of war; crimes against peace; and crimes against humanity. It was from this last category—*crimes against humanity*—that the full criminalization of genocide drew breath and from which the right and obligation of states to intervene in other states when human rights are in jeopardy in other states was established. According to the British Chief Prosecutor at Nuremberg:

> Normally international law concedes that is it for the State to decide how it shall treat its own nationals; it is a matter of domestic jurisdiction. . . . Yet, international law has in the past made some claim that there is a limit to the omnipotence of the State and that the individual human being. . . . is entitled to the protection of mankind when the State tramples upon its rights in a manner that outrages the conscience of mankind. . . . The fact is that the right of humanitarian intervention by war is not a novelty in international law—can intervention by judicial process then be illegal?[1]

In creating a greatly strengthened antigenocide regime, principal responsibility fell upon the newly formed United Nations. Beginning with a General Assembly definition and resolution in 1946 affirming the lawmaking quality of the Nuremberg judgment and principles, the United Nations went on to complete a Convention on the Prevention and Punishment of the Crime of Genocide on December 9 1948. This Convention, which removes any doubts about the lawlessness of genocide, entered into force (1951) when a sufficient number of signatory states had deposited their instruments of ratification. Curiously, the United States (the Senate) has still not ratified this vital Convention, largely out of a misplaced fear of surrender of sovereignty.[2]

Taken together with other important covenants, treaties, and declarations, the Genocide Convention represents the end of the idea of absolute sovereignty concerning nonintervention when human rights are in grievous jeopardy. The Charter of the United Nations—a multilateral, law-making treaty—stipulates in its Preamble and several articles that human rights are protected by international law. This stipulation was reaffirmed by major covenants in 1966 and by the Helsinki Final Act in 1975. Of course, the UN's Universal Declaration of Human Rights (1948) must also be considered an integral part of the antigenocide regime. Although this Declaration is not, strictly speaking, a law-making document, it does articulate "the general principles of law recognized by civilized nations" (a proper source of international law under Article 38 of the Statute of the International Court of Justice), and it does represent an authoritative elucidation of the law of the Charter.

The UN Charter contains many important provisions concerning the protection of human rights. In the Preamble, the peoples of the United Nations reaffirm their faith "in fundamental human rights, in the dignity and worth of the human person, in the equal rights of men and women and of nations large and small" and their determination "to promote social progress and better standards of life in larger freedom."

Article 1 lists a main purpose of the UN as "promoting and encouraging respect for human rights and for fundamental freedoms for all without distinction as to race, sex, language or religion." Similarly, in Article 55, the Charter seeks "universal respect for, and observance of, human rights and fundamental freedoms for all without distinction of race, sex, language or religion." And in Article 56, all Members of the United Nations "pledge themselves to take joint and separate action in cooperation with the Organization for the achievement of the purposes set forth in Article 55."

The UN's Universal Declaration of Human Rights has been used to justify various actions by the organization; to justify various human rights conventions and to exert influence on various national constitutions. For example, when the International Covenants were adopted by the General

Assembly on December 16, 1966, the provisions of the Declaration were effectively transformed into international *conventional* law.

In promoting human rights, various special responsibilities devolve upon specific organs of the United Nations. Under Article 13 of the Charter, one function of the General Assembly is to assist "in the realization of human rights and fundamental freedoms for all without distinction as to race, sex, language or religion." In addition to referring human rights matters to certain permanent committees, the General Assembly has, from time to time, established subsidiary organs of an ad hoc character (e.g., the Special Committee on the Policies of Apartheid of the Government of the Republic of South Africa and the Special Committee on the Situation with Regard to the Implementation of the Declaration on the Granting of Independence to Colonial Countries and Peoples).

Under Article 62 of the Charter, the Economic and Social Council is given certain responsibilities for promoting human rights. Additional responsibilities are conferred by Article 64. The Commission on Human Rights, established in 1946, is one of the fundamental commissions of the Economic and Social Council. Since its inception, the Commission has worked toward submitting proposals, recommendations, and reports to the Council on matters regarding virtually all aspects of human rights. Finally, it should be understood that all of the other primary organs of the UN may from time to time be concerned with the protection of human rights and the prevention of genocide.

In light of these codified expressions of international law, it is abundantly clear that individual states can no longer claim sovereign immunity from responsibility for genocidal treatment of their own citizens. Notwithstanding Article 2(7) of the UN Charter, which reaffirms certain areas of "domestic jurisdiction," each state is now clearly obligated to oppose genocide. Even the failure to ratify specific treaties or conventions (e.g., the United States and the Genocide Convention) does not confer immunity from responsibility, since all states are bound by the law of the Charter and by the customs and general principles of law from which such agreements derive. In the words of President Jimmy Carter before the United Nations on March 17, 1977:

> The search for peace and justice also means respect for human dignity. All the signatories of the United Nations Charter have pledged themselves to observe and respect basic human rights. Thus, no member of the United Nations can claim that mistreatment of its citizens is solely its own business. Equally, no member can avoid its responsibilities to review and to speak when torture or unwarranted deprivation of freedom occurs in any part of the world.

In a very real sense, worldwide unconcern for legal protection of human rights (including, ultimately, genocide) grew out of the post-Westphalian system of world politics—a system that sanctified untrammeled competition between sovereign states and that identified national loyalty as the overriding human obligation. With these developments, unfettered nationalism and state centrism became the dominant characteristics of international relations and the resultant world order came to subordinate all moral and ethical sensibilities to the idea of unlimited sovereignty. Such subordination was more than a little ironic, since even Jean Bodin, who advanced the idea of sovereignty as one free of any external control or internal division, recognized the limits imposed by divine law and natural law.

In the words of the distinguished legal theorist, Charles De Visscher, the growth of positivism "bled white" international law by making the manifested will of the state the sole criterion of validity for norms.[3] Today, however, in the post-Nuremberg world order, we have begun to return to an idea of international law that recognizes its teleological character. Although it is probably unreasonable to claim that we have returned to the classical/medieval idea of natural law's preeminence over all human institutions, the present world order has clearly discarded the notion that the state has its own morality which displaces the notion of human community. This community, as Francisco de Vitoria argued in 1532, remains the fundamental fact against which the fractionation of humanity into smaller units cannot prevail.

Now, what does all of this mean from the point of view of realpolitik and U.S. foreign policy? Granted, there now exists a regime of binding international agreements that places worldwide human welfare above the particularistic interests of individual states or elites, but what can this regime be expected to accomplish? Granted, there are now explicit and codified rules of international law that pertain to genocide, but what can be done about their effective enforcement? Indeed, doesn't a consideration of post–World War II history reveal several instances of genocide (the Cambodian case being perhaps the most far-reaching and abhorrent)? Where was international law?

To answer these questions, one must first recall that international law is a distinctive and unique system of law. This is the case because it is decentralized rather than centralized; because it exists within a social setting (the world political system) that lacks government. It follows that in the absence of central authoritative institutions for the making, interpretaion, and enforcement of law, these juridical processes devolve upon *individual states*. It is, then, the responsibility of individual states, acting alone or in collaboration with other states, to make international law "work" with respect to genocide.

How can this be done? In terms of the law of the Charter, it is essential that states continue to reject the Article 2(7) claim to "domestic jurisdiction" whenever gross outrages against human rights are involved. Of course, the tension between the doctrines of "domestic jurisdiction" and "international concern" is typically determined by judgments of national self-interest, but it would surely be in the long-term interest of all states to oppose forcefully all crimes against humanity. As Vattel observed correctly in the Preface to his *The Law of Nations* in 1758:

> But we know too well from sad experience how little regard those who are at the head of affairs pay to rights when they conflict with some plan by which they hope to profit. They adopt a line of policy which is often false, because often unjust; and the majority of them think that they have done enough in having mastered that. Nevertheless, it can be said of States, what has long been recognized as true of individuals, that the *wisest* and the *safest* policy is one that is founded upon justice.

With this observation Vattel echoes Cicero's contention that "No one who has not the strictest regard for justice can administer public affairs to advantage." But how are we to move from assessment to action, from prescription to policy? Where exactly, is the normative juncture between the legal theory of preventing genocide and the operationalization of that theory?

Under the terms of Article 56 of the Charter, member states are urged to "take joint and separate action in cooperation with the organization" to promote human rights. Reinforced by an abundant body of ancillary prescriptions, this obligation stipulates that the legal community of humankind must allow, indeed *require,* "humanitarian intervention" by individual states in circumstances which involve genocide. Of course, such intervention must not be used as a pretext for aggression and it must conform to settled legal norms governing the use of force, especially the principles of *discrimination, military necessity,* and *proportionality.*[4] Understood in terms of the long-standing distinction between *jus ad bellum* and *jus in bello,* this means that even where the "justness" of humanitarian intervention is clearly established, the means used in that intervention must not be unlimited. As we already know, the lawfulness of a cause does not in itself legitimize the use of certain forms of violence.

As for the legality of humanitarian intervention (*jus ad bellum*), it has been well-established for a long time. Although it has been strongly reinforced by the post-Nuremberg human rights regime, we may find support for the doctrine in Grotius' seventeenth-century classic, *The Law of War and Peace.*[5] Here, the idea is advanced and defended that states may interfere within the territorial sphere of validity of other states to protect innocent persons from their own rulers, an idea nurtured and sustained by the natural law origins of international law:

> There is also another question, whether a war for the subjects of another be just, for the purpose of defending them from injuries inflicted by their ruler. Certainly it is undoubted that ever since civil societies were formed, the ruler each claimed some especial right over his own subjects. Euripides makes his characters say that they are sufficient to right wrongs in their own city. And Thucydides puts among the marks of empire, the supreme authority in judicial proceedings. And so Virgil, Ovid and Euripides in the *Hippolytus*. This is, as Ambrose says, that peoples may not run into wars by usurping the care for those who do not belong to them. The Corinthians in Thucydides say that it is right that each state should punish its own subjects. And Perseus says that he will not plead in defense of what he did against the Dolopians, since they were under his authority and he had acted upon his right. But all this applies when the subjects have really violated their duty; and we may add, when the case is doubtful. . . . But the case is different if the wrong be manifest. If a tyrant like Busiris, Phalaris, Diomede of Thrace practices atrocities toward his subjects, which no just man can approve, the right of human social connection is not cut off in such a case.[6]

This idea is supported by Vattel's argument in *The Law of Nations* (1758):

> Nations have obligations to produce welfare and happiness in other states. In the event of civil war, for example, states must aid the party "which seems to have justice on its side" or protect an unfortunate people from an unjust tyrant.[7]

While the theory of international law still oscillates between an individualist conception of the state and a universalist conception of humanity, the post–World War II regime of treaties, conventions, and declarations that seeks to prevent genocide is necessarily founded upon a broad doctrine of humanitarian intervention. Indeed, it is the very purpose of this regime to legitimize an "allocation of competences" that favors the natural rights of humankind over any particularistic interests of state. Since the prevention of genocide is now undeniably within the ambit of global responsibility, the subjectivism of state primacy has been unambiguously subordinated to the enduring primacy of international justice. In place of the Hegelian concept of the state as an autonomous, irreducible center of authority (because it is an ideal that is the perfect manifestation of Mind), there is now in force a greatly expanded version of the idea of "international concern." In the words of Messrs. McDougal, Lasswell, and Chen:

> The general community is made competent to inquire into how a particular state treats, not merely aliens, but all individuals within its boundaries, including its own nationals. Indeed, given the facts of global interdependence[8] and the intimate links between peace and human rights, much of humankind appears today to have come to the opinion that nothing could be of greater "international concern" than the "human rights" of all individuals.[9]

The starting point for Messrs. McDougal, Lasswell and Chen is the following expression of normative objective:

> The observational standpoint to which we aspire is that of citizens of the larger community of humankind who identify with the whole community, rather than with the primacy of particular groups, and who are committed to clarifying and securing the common interests of all individuals in realizing human dignity on the widest possible scale.[10]

As we have already seen, this starting point is not associated with a new understanding of international law but with a reformulation and refinement of the long-standing idea of universality and reason. And this long-standing idea is nurtured not only by the great text-writers on jurisprudential thought, but also by the major historic movements for human freedom and human dignity, including the English, American, French, Russian, and Chinese revolutions.

Within the current system of international law, external decision makers are authorized to intercede in certain matters that might at one time have been regarded as internal to a particular state. Whereas, at certain times in the past, even gross violations of human rights were defended by appeal to "domestic jurisdiction," today's demands for exclusive competence must be grounded in far more than an interest in avoiding intervention. This trend in authoritative decision making toward an expansion of the doctrine of "international concern" has been clarified by Lauterpacht's definition of intervention:

> Intervention is a technical term of, on the whole, unequivocal connotation. It signifies dictatorial interference in the sense of action amounting to a denial of the independence of the State. It implies a demand which, if not complied with, involves a threat of, or recourse to, compulsion, though not necessarily physical compulsion, in some form.[11]

We can see, therefore, that intervention is not always impermissible, and that—indeed—any assessment of its lawfulness must always be contingent upon *intent*. Applying Lauterpacht's standard, it follows that where there is no interest in exerting "dictatorial interference," but simply an overriding commitment to prevent genocide, the act of intervening may represent the proper enforcement of pertinent legal norms. This concept of intervention greatly transforms the exaggerated emphasis on domestic jurisdiction that has been associated improperly with individual national interpretations of Article 2(7) of the UN Charter and, earlier, with Article 15(8) of the Covenant of the League of Nations. By offering a major distinction between the idea of self-serving interference by one state in the internal affairs of another state and the notion of the general global community's inclusive application of law to the protection of human life and dignity, it significantly advances the goal of a viable antigenocide regime.

The importance of the changing doctrine of intervention to the shift in global "allocation of competences" was prefigured by the *Tunis–Morocco* case before the Permanent Court of International Justice in 1923. In this case, the Court developed a broad test to determine whether or not a matter is essentially within the domestic jurisdiction of a particular state:

> The question whether a certain matter is or is not solely within the domestic jurisdiction of a state is an essentially relative question: it depends upon the development of international relations.

Although this test is hardly free of ambiguity, it does clarify that the choice between "international concern" and "domestic jurisdiction" is not grounded in unalterable conditions of fact, but rather in constantly changing circumstances that permit a continuing adjustment of competences. It follows that whenever particular events create a significant threat of genocide, the general global community is entitled to internationalize jurisdiction and to authorize appropriate forms of decision and action.

Where conditions are judged to permit "humanitarian intervention," say McDougal and his associates, the general community "may enter into the territory of the defaulting state for the purposes of terminating the outrage and securing compliance with a minimum international standard of human rights."[12] This doctrine of humanitarian intervention echoes E. Borchard's prior formulation in 1922:

> Where a state under exceptional circumstances disregards certain rights of its own citizens, over whom presumably it has absolute sovereignty, the other states of the family of nations are authorized by international law to intervene on grounds of humanity. When the "human rights" are habitually violated, one or more states may intervene in the name of the society of nations and may take such measures as to substitute at least temporarily, if not permanently, its own sovereignty for that of the state thus controlled. Whatever the origin, therefore, of the rights of the individual, it seems assured that these essential rights rest upon the ultimate sanction of international law and will be protected, in last resort, by the most appropriate organ of the international community.[13]

Ironically, the United Nations, which is responsible for most of the post-Nuremberg codification of the international law of human rights, has sometimes been associated with increased limits on the doctrine of humanitarian intervention. These limits, of course, flow from the greatly reduced justification for the use of force in the UN Charter's system of international law, especially the broad prohibition contained in Article 2(4). Yet, while it cannot be denied that humanitarian intervention might be used as a pretext for naked aggression, it is also incontestable that a too literal interpretation of 2(4) would summarily destroy the entire corpus of normative protection against genocide—a corpus that is coequal with "peace" as the central objective of the Charter. Moreover, in view of the important nexus between peace and human rights, a nexus in which the former is very much dependent upon widespread respect for human dignity, a too literal interpretation of 2(4) might well impair the prospects for long-term security. This is the case, as McDougal and others have correctly observed, because "the use of armed force in defense of human rights may be emphatically in the common interest as a mode of maintaining international peace and security."[14]

It must be widely understood that the Charter does not prohibit all uses of force and that certain uses are clearly permissible in pursuit of basic human rights. Notwithstanding its attempt to bring greater centralization to legal processes in world politics, the Charter system has not impaired the long-standing right of individual states to act on behalf of the international legal order. In the continuing absence of effective central authoritative processes for decision and enforcement, the legal community of humankind must continue to allow, indeed, must continue to *require,* humanitarian intervention by individual states.

Taken together with an abundant body of ancillary prescriptions concerning human rights and with the full measure of appropriate customs, general principles and text-writings (including, of course, the natural law foundations of international law) the Charter has rendered the norm of absolute nonintervention sterile and void. Rejecting the view that each state is totally free to regulate its affairs without interference by other states (Article 56, for example, obligates member states to "take joint and separate action in cooperation with the Organization" on behalf of human rights), the UN system of international law now condones and *expects* corrective interventions whenever genocide is taking place.

The actual practice of humanitarian intervention on behalf of beleaguered citizens of other states has ample precedent, prefiguring even the current world legal order. One of the earliest recorded cases of such intervention concerns an event that took place in 480 B.C., when Gelon, Prince of Syracuse, after defeating the Carthaginians, demanded as one of the conditions of peace that they abandon the custom of sacrificing their children to Saturn. In the nineteenth century, the high point of positivist jurisprudence, the humanitarian intervention of Great Britain, France, and Russia in 1827 was designed to end Turkey's particularly inhumane methods against the Greek struggle for independence. Similar aims, *inter alia,* provoked U.S. intervention in the Cuban Civil War in 1898. Ironically, perhaps (in light of post-World War II relations between the United States and Cuba), this intervention was intended to put an end, in the words of the joint resolution of April 20, 1898, to "the abhorrent conditions which have existed for more than three years in the island of Cuba; have shocked the moral sense of the people of the United States, have been a disgrace to Christian civilization."

Other cases come to mind as well. In 1902, on the occasion of persecution of Jews in Rumania, the United States—although not a signatory of the Articles of the Treaty of Berlin (protecting the Balkan minorities), made a case for humanitarian intervention. If, said Secretary of State Hay, the United States was not entitled to invoke the clauses of the Treaty, "it must insist upon the principles therein set forth, because these are principles of law and eternal justice."[15]

As we have seen, humanitarian intervention is one way of giving effect to the enforcement of antigenocide norms in international law. Another way involves the use of courts, domestic and international. Under Article V of the Genocide Convention, signatory states are required to enact "the necessary legislation to give effect to" the Convention. Article VI of that Convention further provides that trials for its violation be conducted "by a competent tribunal of the State in the territory of which the act was committed, or by any such international penal tribunal as may have jurisdiction."

Here, there are some special problems. First, apart from the European Human Rights Court at Strasbourg, no such international penal tribunal has been established. The International Court of Justice at the Hague has no penal or criminal jurisdiction.

The International Court of Justice (ICJ) does, however, have jurisdiction over disputes concerning the interpretation and application of a number of specialized human rights conventions. Such jurisdiction is accorded by the Genocide Convention (Article 9); the Supplementary Convention on the Abolition of Slavery; the Slave Trade and Institutions and Practices Similar to Slavery (1956, Article 10); the Convention on the Political Rights of Women (1953, Article 9); the Convention Relating to the Status of Refugees (1951, Article 38); and the Convention on the Reduction of Statelessness (1961, Article 14). In exercising its jurisdiction, however, the ICJ must still confront significant difficulties in bringing recalcitrant states into contentious proceedings. There is still no way to effectively ensure the attendance of defendant states before the Court. Although many states have acceded to the Optional Clause of the Statute of the ICJ (Article 36, Paragraph 2), these accessions are watered down by many attached reservations.

Second, courts of the states where acts in violation of the Genocide Convention have been committed are hardly likely to conduct proceedings against their own national officials (excluding, of course, the possibility of courts established following a coup d'état or revolution). What is needed, therefore, is an expansion of the practice of states after World War II—a practice by states that had been occupied during the war—of seeking extradition of criminals and of trying them in their own national courts.

Let us briefly review the basic contours of this practice:

After the Second World War, three judicial solutions were adapted to the problem of determining the proper jurisdiction for trying Nazi offenses by the victim states, solutions that were additional to the specially constituted Nuremberg Tribunal.

The first solution involved the creation of special courts set up expressly for the purpose at hand. This solution was adopted in Rumania, Czechoslovakia, Holland, Austria, Bulgaria, Hungary, and Poland.

The second solution, adopted in Great Britain, Australia, Canada, Greece, and Italy, involved the establishment of special military courts.

The third solution brought the Nazis and their collaborators before ordinary courts—a solution accepted in Norway, Denmark and Yugoslavia. This solution was adopted by Israel although, strictly speaking, the State of Israel did not exist at the time of the commission of the crimes in question.

In the future, I would suggest that there need be no war or occupation to justify the use of domestic courts to punish crimes of genocide. There is nothing novel about such a suggestion since a principal purpose of the Genocide Convention lies in its explicit applicability to nonwartime actions. Limits upon actions against enemy nationals are as old as the laws of war of international law. But the laws of war do not cover a government's actions against its own nationals. It is, therefore, primarily in the area of domestic atrocities that the Genocide Convention seeks to expand preexisting international penal law.

Going beyond Article VI of the Genocide Convention, which holds to the theory of "concurrent jurisdiction" (jurisdiction based on the site of the alleged offense and on the nationality of the offender), *any* state may now claim jurisdiction when the crime involved is genocide. There is already ample precedent for such a rule in international law, a precedent based upon the long-standing treatment of "common enemies of mankind" (*hostes humani generis*) or international outlaws as within the scope of "universal jurisdiction." In Vattel's 1758 classic, *The Law of Nations,* the following argument is advanced:

> While the jurisdiction of each State is in general limited to punishing crimes committed in its territory, an exception must be made against those criminals who, by the character and frequency of their crimes, are a menace to public security everywhere and proclaim themselves enemies of the whole human race. Men who are by profession poisoners, assassins, or incendiaries may be exterminated wherever they are caught; for they direct their disastrous attacks against all Nations, by destroying the foundations of their common safety.[16]

Vattel's argument echoes the sixth century A.D. *Corpus Juris Civilis* (especially Chapter III, 15, *"ubi de criminibus agi oportet"*) and Grotius'

The Law of War and Peace (especially Book II, Ch. 20). It also parallels the whole corpus of cases, since antiquity, involving piracy (*hostes humani generis*) and is built into the four Geneva Conventions of August 12, 1949, which unambiguously impose upon the High Contracting Parties the obligation to punish certain grave breaches of their rules, regardless of where the infraction is committed or the nationality of the authors of the crime in question (see Article 49 of Convention No. 1; Article 50 of Convention No. 2; Article 129 of Convention No. 3; and Article 146 of Convention No. 4). Most important, the post–Nuremberg international legal order obligates states to recognize universal jurisdiction in punishing crimes against humanity. Such punishment directly concerns each state since fundamental human rights have now been consecrated by international law as an imperious postulate of the general community of humankind. By acting in compliance with this postulate, each state protects the interests of this entire community at the same time as it safeguards its own interests.

The case of universal jurisdiction in matters concerning genocide is further strengthened by the difficulties surrounding extradition. The best example is the case of Israel in the apprehension, trial, and punishment of Adolph Eichmann. In 1950 Israel enacted the Nazis and Nazi Collaborators Punishment Law. In this enactment Israel did nothing different than other states that had been occupied during the war, although of course the State of Israel did not exist at the time of the commission of the crimes.[17] Yet its subsequent efforts to obtain certain major war criminals (e.g., Joseph Mengele) from Argentina and elsewhere via extradition were improperly rebuffed.

Why were the refusals to extradite contrary to international law? For the most part these refusals were grounded in the argument that the crimes in question were of a "political nature." Although there is a "political offense" exception to the international law of extradition, this exception is explicitly precluded by the Genocide Convention in cases involving crimes against humanity. Moreover, under the formula, extradite or prosecute, the states refusing extradition were obligated to prosecute the alleged offenders themselves. Needless to say, no attempts at prosecution were ever undertaken. Finally, these refusals to extradite were contrary to long-standing principles of international law as elucidated by the teachings and writings of highly qualified publicists. According to Vattel, for example:

> If the sovereign of the country in which the crimes of this nature [crimes involving "common enemies of mankind"] have been committed requests the surrender of the perpetrators for the purpose of punishing them, they should be turned over to him as being the one who has first interest in inflicting exemplary punishment upon them; and as it is proper that the guilty should be convicted after a trial conducted with due process of law, we have another reason why criminals of this class are ordinarily delivered up to the States in which the crimes have been committed.[18]

Yet, Vattel recognized that extradition could not always be expected and that the interests of justice could be served only through the universalization of jurisdiction on matters concerning *hostes humani generis.* Thus, he also understood that "pirates are hanged by the first persons into whose hands they fall."[19] On such reasoning, Israel's secret service (*Mossad*) abducted Eichmann in Buenos Aires and transported him to Jerusalem for trial and, ultimately, execution. Had it not acted on the correct principle of universal jurisdiction, Eichmann would almost surely never have been brought to trial for the offenses he committed.

During the time that the abduction and trial took place, there was no longer any legal or technical difficulty with the idea of crimes against humanity (or its derivative, "crimes against the Jewish people") since the issues of retroactivity, superior orders and *tu quoque* had already been resolved at Nuremberg.

With respect to the issue of retroactivity, Nuremberg established that there had been operative certain principles of *positive* law at the time of the crimes (the laws of war, international custom, the general principles of law recognized by civilized nations, and the writings of scholars) and of *natural law.* Moreover, the Tribunal concluded that retroactivity need not be unjust and that, indeed, its application might be necessary to the interests of justice. In the words of the Tribunal, "So far from it being unjust to punish him, it would be unjust if his wrongs were allowed to go unpunished"—*nullum crimen sine poena.*

In rendering its judgment on Adolph Eichmann, the Israeli court built upon this reaffirmation of natural law, noting that there may be special occasions and circumstances for which the law, for want of foresight, failed to make provision. Moreover, citing an important case from English law, the Israeli court offered a vital conceptual distinction between retroactive law and ex post facto law. Drawn from Blackstone's *Commentaries,* this distinction held that "ex post facto laws are objectionable when, after an action indifferent in itself is committed, the legislator then, for the first time, declares it to have been a crime and inflicts a punishment upon the person who has committed it. . . . Here it is impossible that the party could foresee that an action, innocent when it was done, should afterwards be converted to guilt by subsequent law. He had, therefore, no cause to abstain from it and all punishment for not abstaining must, in consequence, be cruel and unjust." In the Eichmann case, of course, the laws involved did not create a new crime and it certainly could not be said that he did not have criminal intent (*mens rea*). The accused's actions were hardly "indifferent," and they were assuredly considered crimes, at the time of their commission, by all civilized nations.

With respect to the issue of superior orders, the classical writers on international law had long rejected that doctrine as a proper defense against the charge of war crimes. The German code of military law operative during the war provided that a soldier must execute all orders undeterred by the fear of legal consequences, but it added that this would not excuse him in cases where he must have known with certainty that the order was illegal. This view was upheld in an important decision of the German Supreme Court in Leipzig in 1921. According to the Court, a subordinate who obeyed the order of his superior officer was liable to punishment if it were known to him that such an order involved a contravention of international law.

The defense of "superior orders" was also rejected at the Einsatzgruppen trial undertaken by an American military tribunal. According to the tribunal: "The obedience of a soldier is not the obedience of an automaton. A soldier is a reasoning agent. It is a fallacy of widespread consumption that a soldier is required to do everything his superior officers order him to do. The subordinate is bound only to obey the lawful orders of his superior."

Ironically, Goebbels himself spoke against the plea of superior orders during the war. In an article in the German press on May 28, 1944, he wrote: "No international law of warfare is in existence which provides that a soldier who has committed a mean crime can escape punishment by pleading as his defense that he followed the commands of his superiors. This holds particularly true if those commands are contrary to all human ethics and opposed to the well-established international usage of warfare." It was the bombing of Germany by the allies to which Goebbels referred, and he was attempting to justify the Nazi practice of shooting captured Allied airmen.

With respect to the issue of *tu quoque,* it was irrelevant in Jerusalem since Israel had obviously not been a belligerent during World War II. Hence, it was logically impossible that its capacity to sit in judgment over Eichmann would have been compromised by any misdeeds of its own.

It follows from this discussion that Israel's trial of Adolph Eichmann was fully consistent with the post-Nuremberg imperatives of international law and that its jurisdiction in the matter flowed properly from the universal nature of the crime and from the particular suffering of the Jewish people. The crimes set forth by Israeli law (namely crimes of war and crimes against humanity) had been unambiguously established as crimes by the Nuremberg Tribunal and the human rights regime derivative from that Tribunal. The special charge of crimes against the Jewish people derived properly from the principle of "sovereign equality" and from Israel's inherent right as a state (albeit constituted after the war) to punish those who would do it harm. This special charge also derived properly from the overriding imperatives of natural law.

All of the crimes set forth under the Israeli indictment had therefore been recognized by the universal conscience of mankind and by its institutionalized legal expressions as being *delicta juris gentium* (crimes of international law). And since an international tribunal that might have judged these crimes did not, for the moment, exist (Nuremberg, it should be noted, dealt only with "humanity," and not with "the Jewish People"), Israel properly invested its legislative and judicial organs of state with the power of enforcement. In so doing, it acted upon the well-established practice that each state reserves the right to punish a crime that is a violation of the norms of the law of nations, regardless of the place in which the deed was committed or the nationality of the accused or of the victim. In acting to punish the crime of genocide, Israel acted to safeguard not only its own interests, but also the interests of the entire community of humankind. By acting upon the principle of universal jurisdiction, it established beyond any reasonable doubt that the punishment of genocide is not an internal question for each state but a peremptory obligation of humankind.

In terms of the broad issue of using domestic courts to uphold international law, the example of the United States is of particular interest. Since its founding, the United States has reserved the right to enforce international law within its own courts. Article I, Section 8, Clause 10 of the American Constitution confers on Congress the power "to define and punish piracies and felonies committed on the high seas, and offenses against the law of nations." Pursuant to this constitutional prerogative, the first Congress, in 1789, passed the Alien Tort Statute. This statute authorizes U.S. federal courts to hear those civil claims by aliens alleging acts committed "in violation of the law of nations or a treaty of the United States" when the alleged wrongdoers can be found in the United States. At that time, of course, the particular target of this legislation was piracy on the high seas.

Over the years, U.S. federal courts have rarely invoked the "law of nations," and then only in such cases where the acts in question had already been proscribed by treaties or conventions. In 1979 a case seeking damages for foreign acts of torture was filed in the federal courts. In a complaint filed jointly with his daughter, Dolly, Dr. Joel Filartiga, a well-known Paraguayan physician and artist and an opponent of President Alfredo Stroessner's repressive regime, alleged that members of that regime's police force had tortured and murdered his son, Joelito. On June 30, 1980 the Court of Appeals for the Second Circuit found that since an international consensus condemning torture has crystallized, torture violates the law of nations for purposes of the Alien Tort Statute. U.S. courts, it was held, therefore have jurisdiction under the statute to hear civil suits by the victims of foreign torture, if the alleged international outlaws are found in the United States.[20]

Although this case was a civil suit brought by a dissident against a representative of the Paraguayan regime, the court held, in effect, that torture is a violation of the law of nations and can be redressed in U.S. courts. More recently a unit of the UN Human Rights Commission has been working toward a treaty that would establish a universal criminal jurisdiction especially for torturers—an idea that could ultimately be extended to perpetrators of genocide.

The obligation of U.S. courts to identify and punish gross violations of international law concerning genocide is roughly analogous to these courts' traditional role in redressing deprivations of civil liberties that occur at home. Judge Irving R. Kaufman, who wrote the opinion of the Court on *Filartiga,* noted that parallels can be drawn between *Filartiga* and the Supreme Court's ruling on *Brown* v *Mississippi,* in which murder convictions based on confessions made during torture were declared unconstitutional. Although the United States is reluctant to enter overseas disputes between foreign nationals—just as federal courts hesitate to interfere with state court findings—Judge Kaufman expressed his belief that federal courts should act in cases involving torture, both on the international and the state level. He stated that federal courts have the same obligation to rule on the precepts of international law that they have for constitutional law, in order to uphold the U.S. "commitment to the preservation of fundamental elements of human dignity throughout the world."[21]

With this in mind, it would be enormously useful in reference to the crime of genocide if the United States were to expand its commitment to identify and punish such crimes within its own court structure.

We all know, however, that the United States is typically animated by forces other than an acutely moral imagination and that the presumed requirements of realpolitik invariably take precedence over those of international law. It follows that before the progressive codification of antigenocide norms can be paralleled by the widespread refinement and expansion of pertinent enforcement measures, this country must come to believe that international legal steps to prevent and punish genocide are always in its own best interests. Drawing upon the Thomistic idea of law as a positive force for directing humankind to its proper goals (an idea that is itself derived from Aristotle's conception of the natural development of the state from social impulses), we need to seek ways of aligning the antigenocide dictates of the law of nations with effective strategies of implementation by the United States—that is, strategies based on expanded patterns of humanitarian intervention, transnational judicial settlement, and domestic court involvement.

How may we encourage such an alignment? To answer this question, we must first understand that rationalist philosophy had derived the idea of national sovereignty from the notion of individual liberty, but cast in its post-Westphalian expression, the idea has acted to oppose human dignity and to permit genocide. Left to its own nefarious devices, the legacy of unimpeded nationalism can only be the subordination of all human concerns to the immanent ends of the state. With its objectification of individuals into vast networks of social, economic, and political manipulation, the all-powerful state prods people to accept superstition and chaos.

An important manifestation of this condition is the unwillingness of the United States to intervene on behalf of victims of genocide in other states wherever such intervention is viewed as geopolitically undesirable. Nurtured by a social-Darwinian conception of world politics and by a tenacious commitment to the exigencies of realpolitik, such unwillingness subverts the peremptory obligations of international law and perpetuates the primacy of perceived power over the requirements of justice. The consequences of this debased pattern of international decision making are especially visible today in the context of continuing cold war orientations to foreign affairs—a self-defeating context wherein U.S. policy makers view almost all of their options within the limited parameters of bipolar competition and endless antagonism.

Before the realism of antigenocide ideals can prevail in global society, the United States must learn to escape from the confines of such a limited context for choosing policy options. Under the aegis of present perspectives, we have been willing to abide virtually every evil in the futile search for geopolitical advantage. Indeed, the desolate intuitions of realpolitik have even led the United States to support the murderous forces of Pol Pot as the lawful government of Cambodia.

With such support the United States undermines its interests as well as its ideals. In the years ahead, a continuation of such kinds of support will make it impossible for this country to retain any credible claim to the position of "leader of the free world." Although such a continuation could be reconciled with the claim of reliable opposition to all Marxist regimes, it is no longer reasonable or persuasive to identify such opposition with an affirmative stance on human rights.

We must expect more of our country. By its narrowly adversary vision of foreign affairs, the United States consistently obstructs any remaining chances for a decent world society. During the next few years, the consequences of this thoughtless dualism will if uninterrupted, include a far-reaching pattern of global instability, a pattern that will produce not only worldwide economic collapse but also political unrest and dislocation everywhere. To avoid so invidious a fate, the United States need only understand that its interests are best served by doing what is right in all circumstances, irrespective of the seemingly compelling requirements of an East–West ideological schism. Today, this schism is essentially a contrivance, an elaborate fiction sustained not by the imperatives of an informed consciousness but by the delusional expectations of a shallow and sterile leadership elite.

We can do better. By recognizing in this elite an insurmountable incapacity to be more than mediocre, we can begin to reverse its groundless idolatry of conflict with a productive celebration of life. By recognizing ourselves as both a moral and a mortal nation, we can oppose the illusion of benefit from a frenzied and perpetual anti-Sovietism with the true and effectual vision of goodness. The result will be worth the effort. Instead of a pretext for convulsions, a reason for hysterical imprecations against an Evil Empire, American foreign policy can become the instrument of a peaceful and just world order. And while such policy may fall short of a New Jerusalem, it may still constitute a visible hyphen between heaven and earth.

Notes

1. See *The Charter and Judgment of the Nuremberg Tribunal: History and Analysis,* Memorandum submitted by the Secretary-General, United Nations, General Assembly, International Law Commission, Lake Success, N.Y., 1949, p. 71.

2. The Genocide Convention has been before the U.S. Senate since 1949. The Convention was transmitted to the Senate by President Truman on June 16, 1949. Notwithstanding American failure to ratify, it has been in force since January 12, 1951, 90 days after the requisite 20 states had ratified it. With the exception of President Eisenhower, every U.S. president since Truman has endorsed ratification of the Convention. When Great Britain ratified in 1970, the United States remained the only major Western democracy to have refused ratification. The Soviet Union ratified the Convention in 1954.

An argument made in the United States against ratification concerns Article I, section 8, clause 10 of the U.S. Constitution, which confers on Congress the power "to define and punish piracies and felonies committed on the high seas, and offenses against the law of nations." Here it is feared that ratification of the Genocide Convention would represent a usurpation of the legislative power in the United States. In fact, however, Article V of the Genocide Convention specifically contemplates domestic legislative action, especially in the area of prescribing penalties. Hence, the Convention, for the most part, is not self-executing and does not impair the sovereign prerogatives of the United States.

3. See Preface to Charles de Visscher's *Theory and Reality in Public International Law,* translated by P.E. Corbett (Princeton, N.J.: Princeton University Press, 1968).

4. The idea of *proportionality* is contained in the Mosaic *lex talionis,* since it prescribes that an injury should be requited reciprocally, but certainly not with a greater injury. As Aristotle understood the *lex talionis,* it was a law of justice, not of hatred—one eye, not two, for an eye; one tooth, no more, for a tooth.

5. The idea expressed in Article 38 of the Statute of the International

Court of Justice that scholarly writings (of which Grotius's classic is an instance) are a proper source of international law may have its roots in the Jewish tradition that a fellowship of scholars is entrusted with legal interpretation. This idea, of course, diverges from the Jewish tradition in that the Jewish scholars, rather than being actual sources of legal norms, were always bound by the Talmudic imperative, "Whatever a competent scholar will yet derive from the Law, that was already given to Moses on Mount Sinai" (*Jerusalem Megillah IV*). Yet, even this divergence may not be as far-reaching as first supposed, since one view of the norm-making character of scholarly writings on international law is that these writings are never more than exegeses of overriding natural law and that their contributions to the development of international law are always contingent upon being in harmony with reason or "true law."

6. See *The Law of War and Peace,* Book II, Ch. XXV, VIII, 1, 2.

7. See *The Law of Nations,* p. xii.

8. The idea of interdependence between peoples is hardly new. Almost two hundred years ago, Immanuel Kant wrote in *Perpetual Peace:* "The intercourse, more or less close, which has been everywhere steadily increasing between the nations of the earth, has now extended so enormously that a violation of right in one part of the world is felt all over it."

9. See Myres McDougal, Harold Lasswell, and Lung-Chu Chen, *Human Rights and World Public Order: The Basic Policies of an International Law of Human Rights* (New Haven Conn.: Yale University Press, 1980), p. 211.

10. Ibid., Preface, p. xvii.

11. See *International Law and Human Rights,* 1950.

12. See McDougal, Lasswell, and Chen, *Human Rights and World Public Order,* p. 239.

13. See Edwin Borchard, *The Diplomatic Protection of Citizens Abroad or the Law of International Claims* (1922), p. 14.

14. See McDougal, Lasswell, and Chen, *Human Rights and World Public Order,* p. 241.

15. Cited by Charles de Visscher, *Theory and Reality in Public International Law,* p. 127.

16. See Section 233 of Chapter XIX ("One's Country, and Various Matters Relating to It"), *The Law of Nations,* translation of the edition of 1758 by Charles G. Fenwick (New York: Oceana Publications), reprinted in 1964.

17. In response to the issue of Israel's nonexistence at the time of the Holocaust, Gideon Hausner—who prosecuted Adolf Eichmann before the Jerusalem District Court—makes the following point:

> The argument that Israel did not yet exist when the offenses were committed was highly technical. She could certainly, as a member of the family of nations, claim her right to share in the universal jurisdiction over crimes against humanity. Moreover, the State of Israel had grown from the Jewish community in Palestine, which had been internationally recognized since 1917, under the Balfour Declaration and later under the Peace Treaty, which gave it the status of a "Jewish National Home." Palestinian Jews had fought under their own flag in World War II; post-war Israel had been recognized by the Western Allies as having been a cobelligerent and had been invited to join them in terminating the state of war with Western Germany.

(See Hausner's *Justice in Jerusalem* (New York: Schocken Books, 1968), p. 315.

18. See Vattel, *The Law of Nations,* Section 233.

19. Ibid.

20. See Irving R. Kaufman, "A Legal Remedy for International Torture," *New York Times Magazine,* November 9, 1980, p. 52. The author, a judge of the U.S. Court of Appeals for the Second Circuit, wrote the opinion of the Court.

21. Ibid., p. 52.

7 From Paradigm to Planetization: The Journey Begun

In a major work of modern philosophy and social science, *The Structure of Scientific Revolutions,* Thomas S. Kuhn articulates a particularly fruitful concept: the idea of "paradigm."[1] By this concept Kuhn refers to certain examples of scientific practice that provide models for further inquiry—Ptolemaic or Copernican astronomy, Aristotelian dynamics, Newtonian mechanics, and so on. At any given moment in history, the prevailing paradigm within a given discipline defines the basic contours of all investigation. The transformations of these paradigms, transformations occasioned by the incontestable opposition of new facts and empirical findings, are "scientific revolutions," and the transition from one paradigm to another is the manner in which science is able to progress.

Understood in terms of our own concern, the transformation of U.S. foreign policy behavior from a realpolitik to a world order orientation, Kuhn's wisdom suggests the need for a new paradigm of American statecraft. Before the world can change, paradigms must change. Before U.S. foreign policy behavior can create a more auspicious domestic and global pattern of interaction, there must take place a revolution of consciousness.

The impetus for such a revolution is already here. It lies in the crises of world politics, which cannot be resolved within the time-dishonored framework of realpolitik. Faced with this condition, realpolitik must give way to an improved framework for understanding and coping with global political life. Only then, armed with a hopeful paradigm that can give rise to viable strategies of survival, can we hope to endure.

This new paradigm that we seek depends largely on a process of nonincremental or revolutionary changes in thought. Although it is certainly true that all science progresses by accretion, specifically by the continuous accumulation of "failed" hypotheses, it is also true that accretion has never been sufficient. The major episodes within science wherein an overarching approach to the discipline has been replaced by another—as in the advent of Copernicanism, Darwinism, and Einsteinianism—have been *revolutionary* episodes. In a similar fashion the steps that give rise to a new world political dynamic must be founded upon a wholly new understanding of international relations.

Today those who continue to prescribe adherence to the principles of realpolitik are much like the occupants of Plato's cave. Deprived of an illuminating vision of reality, they are destined to live in a world of illusion, animated by distortions that can never impel reasonable behavior. No matter how vigorously they cling to their tenets of "pragmatism," their truth is, as Plato suggests, "literally nothing but the shadows of images."

What will happen if advocates of realpolitik are released from their intellectual captivity and permitted to confront their earlier illusions from a position of genuine lucidity? For a time we may suppose that they would resemble the prisoners Plato describes in Book VII of *The Republic* after they are given freedom to leave the cave:

> At first, when any of them is liberated and compelled suddenly to stand up and turn his neck round and walk and look towards the light, he will suffer sharp pains; the glare will distress him, and he will be unable to see the realities of which in his former state he had seen the shadows; and then conceive someone saying to him, that what he saw before was an illusion, but that now, when he is approaching nearer to being and his eye is turned towards more real existence, he has a clearer vision—what will be his reply? And you may further imagine that his instructor is pointing to the objects as they pass and requiring him to name them—will he not be perplexed? Will he not fancy that the shadows which he formerly saw are truer than the objects which are now shown to him?

"Far truer," says Plato, After a time, however, subtle changes take place. He will grow accustomed to the sight of the "upper world." Although he first saw shadows best, he will soon begin to be disabused of his earlier errors. As a consequence of this transformation, he will begin to challenge the wisdom of the den and to pity his former fellow-prisoners.

Plato's allegory, of course, concerns the upward ascent of the soul from the prison-house of the perceptual world toward the true intellectual world. It is a laborious ascent, and one that defers genuine knowledge until the very last phase. It is also a problematic ascent, since those who succeed in the effort will be disinclined to adapt their vision of reality to human affairs "for their souls are ever hastening into the upper world where they desire to dwell; which desire of theirs is very natural."

Viewed in terms of the need to move beyond realpolitik in U.S. foreign affairs, however, it is an ascent that must be tried. Moreover, those who have made the ascent, those statemen and scholars who have recognized the futility of power politics, must not be allowed to leave the upper world. Rather than descend again among the prisoners in the den, they must be encouraged to share their newfound wisdom with others in the realm of public affairs.

Before all of this can take place, we will require a broad-based popular movement of national and international dimensions. Founded upon a thorough rejection of realpolitik and invested with a commitment to transform self-defeating political and military strategies, this movement could begin to nurture an informed cadre of political leaders. In the final analysis, however, the creation of such a movement will itself require antecedent transformations of educational structures and processes, transformations that subordinate the rampant vocationalism and skills-orientation of the present to a human-centered system of personal growth and interpersonal harmony.

The end of realpolitik requires an expanded awareness of global solidarity. Each person must renew his or her awareness of oneness or connectedness. Each person's future is tied intimately to the whole. All people are linked to their fellows and to the larger universe of which they are a part. There are no unrelated beings.

The tradition of human unity and cosmopolis has a long and persuasive history. The great Roman Stoic, Marcus Aurelius, understood the universe as one living being with one substance and all people as actors within a web of single texture. In the words of *Meditations:* "What is the nature of the whole, and what is my nature, and how is this related to that, and what kind of part is it of what kind of whole?" These are the questions that must give direction to each human life.

By the Middle Ages, the idea of universality had fused with the idea of a *respublica Christiana,* a Christian Commonwealth, and Thomas, John of Salisbury, and Dante were contemplating Europe as a unified Christian community. According to Dante's work of 1310, *De Monarchia,* only in its relation to the entire universe could the world be conceived as part rather than whole:

> Further, the whole human race is a whole with reference to certain parts, and, with reference to another whole, it is a part. For it is a whole with reference to particular kingdoms and nations, as we have shown; and it is a part with reference to the whole universe, as is manifest without argument.

This whole universe was tidy and orderly. At its center lay the Earth, at once both a mere part of creation and a single, unified whole unto itself. Such a conception of human oneness lay at the foundations of Emeric Crucé's *The New Cyneas* (1623) and ultimately set the stage for the cosmopolitanism of the German Enlightenment typified by Lessing's *Nathan the Wise* and reaffirmed by the romantic holists, Herder and Goethe.

Recently the writings of Pierre Teilhard de Chardin appear in this tradition. These are rooted in the distinguished Jesuit palaeontologist's concept of "complexification," the process whereby subatomic units pass along to constitute increasingly elaborate systems of social organization. As suggested in *The Phenomenon of Man,* originally published in French in 1955, "Each element of the cosmos is positively woven from all the others." There is no way in which the network of cosmic matter can be sliced up into distinct, isolable units. Only one way of considering the universe is really possible, that is, "to take it as a whole, in one piece."

From the overarching singularity of his kind, man may learn that positive transformation requires an "opening out" to something beyond himself. This singularity does not oppose the enriching function of differentiation, but it does point to an ordering of objectives in which confluence and convergence are uppermost. Whether or not we can actually conceive of a moment in which all peoples will consolidate and complete one another, humankind's task must center about cohesion. Its future requires the understanding that any ramification is subordinate to the aim of coming together. It must, as Chardin tells us, learn to understand the processes involved in the idea of a worldwide totalization of human consciousness, an idea associated with a closed grouping of people:

> Mankind, born on this planet and spread over its entire surface, coming gradually to form around its earthly matrix a single, major organic unity, enclosed upon itself; a single, hypercomplex, hyperconcentrated, hyperconscious arch-molecule, coextensive with the heavenly body on which it is born.

Indeed, says Chardin, this is already happening with "the closing of the spherical, thinking circuit."

With respect to the potential evolutionary future and prospect of the human race, we are born into a world of inconscience. But we are capable of an upward development of consciousness and an ascent into reaches wherein personal growth is easily harmonized with the good of the whole. To unleash this capacity we must appreciate that a oneness lies hidden beneath the diversities of a seemingly fractionated world. People are cemented to one another not by haphazard aggregation, but by the certainty of their basic likeness and by their increasing interdependence.

We can readily see that what is necessary is also improbable, especially in the near future. Even from the point of view of the United States, a state whose doctrinal foundations in natural law suggest a unique capacity for cosmopolitan thinking, there are overwhelming obstacles to be considered. The idea of Manifest Destiny, an idea that historian Henry Steele Commager says was "more manifest to the Americans who profited from it than to the native inhabitants who were its victims," has yet to be effectively repudiated.[2] Although it is no longer fashionable to rationalize foreign intervention in terms of a divine mandate to bring enlightenment to benighted populations, such thinking still underlies a great measure of U.S. foreign policy.

To a significant extent, the legacy of slavery in the United States has also contributed to racism and imperialism abroad. Current U.S. policies in

Asia and Central America and Africa draw sustenance from earlier ventures to assume the civilizing "burdens" of an advanced people. Perhaps we should recall the soldier's song of this country's three-year war against the Filipinos fighting for their independence at the end of the last century:

> Damn, damn, damn the Filipinos
> Slant-eyed kakiack ladrones
> And beneath the starry flag
> Civilize them with a krag
> And return us to our own beloved homes.[3]

These are hardly the verses of a cosmopolitan people. And although such songs are no longer a part of an officially sanctioned repertoire in overseas ventures, the spirit of these ventures persists. Reinforced by unstated notions of natural selection, current U.S. policies continue to turn on the presumption of an innate American superiority.

U.S. commitment to realpolitik certainly antedates *The Origin of Species.* But once that book was published in 1859 it provided yet another justification for race theory and militarism. Indeed, the spirit of Darwinism sustained the belief in Anglo-Saxon racial superiority, which was a dominant tradition of U.S. imperialism. Seizing upon Darwin's idea that the backward races would most likely disappear before the advance of higher civilizations, U.S. militarists could smugly identify their policies as a scientific imperative of natural selection.

Consider, for example, the comments of the Reverend Josiah Strong, whose book *Our Country: Its Possible Future and Its Present Crisis* appeared in 1885 and quickly sold 175,000 copies in English alone. Decribing a situation wherein an expanding global population would soon press upon the carrying capacity of the United States, Strong declared:

> Then will the world enter upon a new stage of its history—*the final competition of races for which the Anglo-Saxon is being schooled.* If I do not read amiss, this powerful race will move down upon Mexico, down upon Central and South America, out upon the islands of the sea, over upon Africa and beyond. And can anyone doubt that the result of this competition of races will be the "survival of the fittest."[4]

Consider, also, the statement of Senator Albert T. Beveridge before the U.S. Senate in 1899, during the fight for the annexation of the Philippines:

> God has not been preparing the English-speaking and Teutonic peoples for a thousand years for nothing but vain and idle self-admiration. No! He has

> made us the master organizers of the world to establish system where chaos reigns. . . . He has made us adept in government that we may administer government among savages and senile peoples.[5]

From such thinking it was only a short step to talk about the menace of the "dark races," "Yellow Peril," and the Vietcong.

In his analysis of Proust, Samuel Beckett says: "Yesterday is not a milestone that has been passed, but a daystone on the beaten track of the years, and irremediably part of us, within us, heavy and dangerous." In terms of this country's capacity to turn from the self-destructive dynamics of realpolitik to a cosmopolitan worldview, Beckett's observation suggests overwhelming difficulty. Since current policies reflect long-standing commitments to militaristic and racist nationalism, their transformation can only take place slowly, bit by bit.

But such transformation *can* happen. In fact, it is already happening. The prejudiced and jingoistic elements of our foreign policy behavior, while still not completely eradicated, have been relegated to the whisperings of back-room conversation. They can no longer be uttered openly in public offices or legislative chambers.

If momentum can be maintained, and vocationalism in education can be tempered by the overriding exigencies of human-centered education, there is reason to hope that purposeless competition and conflict will give way to commonality and communion. In this connection Americans must learn to associate real freedom with a willingness and capacity to disobey. As long as we continue to defer to public authorities in matters of high politics, especially matters of peace and human rights, the prospect of a liberating popular movement against realpolitik will remain distant and remote.

From the point of view of conventional wisdom and political socialization, this assessment must seem manifestly unorthodox. After all, haven't we all been reared with the idea that national interests are always best defined by our authoritative public officials, and that these interests must be accepted under almost all circumstances? Indeed we have! But this idea contradicts every essential feature of our founding ideology, a system of political beliefs that makes the correctness of every political decision contingent on compliance with a Higher Law, one that is universal in scope and discoverable by each individual person. It follows, as we have already seen, that a broadened willingness and capacity to disobey is consistent with the truest principles of Americanism.

At first, the retreat from unquestionning deference to public authority will be slow and halting. As Erich Fromm has recognized, humankind is always prone to obey because obedience makes one part of the whole and thus confers strength: "I can make no error, since it [the power one worships] decides for me; I cannot be alone, because it watches over me; I cannot commit a sin, because it does not let me do so; and even if I do sin, the punishment is only the way of returning to the almighty power."[6] But the retreat is already underway, animated by an expanding awareness of Vietnam and the desolate aftermath for U.S. foreign policy.

This retreat is also animated by the increasingly apparent inability of the state to provide even the most essential elements of security in the nuclear age. Among the major theorists of sovereignty, especially Bodin, Hobbes, and Leibniz, it was always understood that the provision of security is the first obligation of the state. If the modern state can no longer provide such security, it can no longer justify claims of reflexive obedience.

Ironically, therefore, the ever-expanding realm of insecurity in the world can be expected to encourage *intra*national disobedience and ultimately a worldwide public movement against realpolitik. With such expansion, more and more people can be expected to accept the view of Leibniz that the community of greatest significance for each individual person is "not of a particular nation," but rather "the state of the universe."[7] At the same time, such expansion is itself an overriding threat of modern political life and cannot be exploited for any extended period of time.

Finally, an enlarged willingness to disobey wrongheaded or nefarious foreign policies of the United States has been generated by the curious Manicheanism of current ideology. Although Soviet behavior in world affairs hardly meets the test of "goodness," the alleged contrast between the forces of evil and the forces of good represents little more than a childlike caricature. Looking over the entire record of post-World War II American foreign policy, there is little evidence of a singularly greater commitment to virtue. Perhaps the most striking example of this country's characteristic unconcern for justice and its overall similarity to the Soviet Union in world affairs is the Klaus Barbie affair and all that lies behind it.

Reflecting the primacy of realpolitik, U.S. actions shortly after the war involved the support of Barbie and other Nazi war criminals as highly paid U.S. intelligence informants. At a time when the U.S. was involved as the principal architect of the International Military Tribunal at Nuremberg, a secret U.S. military program known as "Ratline" exploited and shielded the perpetrators of crimes against humanity. All this was done, moreover, at a time when tens of thousands of concentration camp survivors were denied admittance to the United States. If follows that if the Soviet Union is indeed "the focus of evil in the modern world," that evil must be extraordinary if, in contrast, Nazi war criminals are contributors to what is good.

In the fashion of the Soviet Union, of course, the United States has always rejected moral conduct as a purposeful standard of foreign policy behavior. There has never been any significant difference between the two superpowers on this issue. During the next several years, however, the simplemindedness of the caricature of Soviet–American rivalry will become more and more obvious to large numbers of people, occasioning still another rationale for disengagement from a futile policy of realpolitik.

Who is the enemy? What notion of adversarial relationship fuels the fires of realpolitik? At the moment, the answers seem clear. The enemy is the Soviet Union; our relations with that state define the boundaries of the world system's primary axis of conflict. Yet, if the Soviet Union did not exist, our leaders would have to invent it. Otherwise, to whom would we feel superior? To whom would we impute our frustrations, our weaknesses, our failures?

The enemy in world politics must always be concrete. It cannot be an opaque, shifting, protean muddle, so ephemeral that there can be no passionate focal point of hostility. Indeed, the enemy must be opposed passionately, since it is on the plane of passion that realpolitik draws its very meaning. Since they are afraid of reason, states long for impenetrability, and it is in the condition of passion that they can acquire the durability of a stone.

It is also on the plane of passion that we may renounce any expectation from the Soviet Union of a course of conduct that is reasonable and self-interested. Everything is made clear and straightforward if we discern in the Kremlin a metaphysical principle that drives it to do evil under all circumstances. The Soviet Union is free to do evil, not good; it cannot be reformed.

With this view, realpolitik reveals its own insubstantiality. Allegedly the only pragmatic approach to world affairs, it is in fact unremittingly utopian. Since the Soviet Union is assimilable to the spirit of evil, no reconciliation or compromise is possible. Its will is one that commits itself purely, gratuitously to be evil. Through it all evil arrives to bedevil world politics. All global misfortune—crises, wars, famines, revolutions—take place because of its interference.

The American supporter of realpolitik is fearful of discovering that the world is ill-contrived, that there exist many causes of its multiple misfortunes, for then he would be compelled to understand and master a complicated reality. Rather than be burdened with an agonizing problem and responsibility, he localizes all evil in the universe in the Soviet Union. Left unimpeded, however, such Manicheanism will have a self-fulfilling effect, creating the conditions under which one or the other (or both) must be annihilated.

At its heart, the problem is one of individuals. Our leaders can exploit a realpolitik worldview only because it satisfies the particular cravings of people. The anti-Sovietism spawned by realpolitik brings special pleasures. By treating the Soviet Union as a pernicious society, Americans affirm at the same time that *they* belong to an elite, one that is based on goodness. There are no special requirements for membership in this elite, no standards of excellence that need to be met, only citizenship in the United States.

We begin to understand the human roots of realpolitik, roots that are inextricably intertwined with the dynamics of anarchy in interstate relations. The individual in world politics, in this case the individual American, supports a protracted enmity with the Soviet Union largely out of fear of being alone. To this end, he finds the existence of the Soviet adversary absolutely necessary. Small matter that the Soviet Union is essentially a state like his own, comprising people like himself. Since he has chosen to devalue words and reasons at the outset, he is impervious to logic, responding only to the strong emotional benefits of Americanism.

The American who embraces the Manicheanism of realpolitik may readily confess that his Soviet counterpart shares a basic humanity. But this concession costs him nothing, for he has put this quality in parentheses. What matters is that a condition of sustained international enmity overcomes solitariness and mediocrity, that it enobles membership in the herd. This American has chosen to accept anti-Sovietism as an article of faith because that is something one cannot believe alone.

It follows from all this that before the United States can extricate itself from the predatory embrace of realpolitik, individual Americans will need to discover alternative and more authentic sources of reassurance. To a certain extent, as we have already noted, this process is already under way, animated by the manifestly contrived dualism offered by our leaders. Yet the benefits of this process will accrue only to those people who display a measure of political awareness; they will be lost upon many millions of others who are unmoved by reason.

What is to be done about *these* people, for whom the angst of our time is only the newest form of hubris? Although their politics is a lie, confirming a total disjunction between problem and solution, it is a politics that confers far-reaching ego satisfaction and self-esteem. Where are there appropriate substitute forms of such satisfaction?

To answer these questions we must first understand that the journey from civilization to planetization begins by myth and ends in doubt. For this journey to succeed, the individual traveling along the route must learn to substitute a system of uncertainties for what one has always believed, must learn to tolerate and encourage doubt as a replacement for the comforting woes of statism. Induced to live against the grain of our civilization, one may become not only conscious of one's singularity, but satisfied with it. Organically separated from civilization, one becomes aware of the forces that undermine it, forces that offer one last remaining chance for both meaning and survival.

Worn threadbare, militaristic nationalism must cease to be a principal source of meaning. Its replacement, however, must be not only authentic, but equally able to control the intensity with which one feels one's insignificance. To close what Pierre Teilhard de Chardin calls "the spherical thinking circuit," the prisoner of realpolitik must learn to discover personal value in his own accomplishments, in his own private characteristics and contributions. Whatever bestows value and self-esteem, so long as it is not hurtful to others or beholden to nationality, advances the conditions of reason and an improved world order.

None of this is to suggest that realpolitik is "caused" by behavioral or psychological deficiencies, but only that such deficiencies are exploited for political effect in a decentralized international setting. Were the world organized differently, in a fashion without multiple sovereignties and zero-sum perceptions, individual human needs would seek different sources of satisfaction. In such a world there could be no realpolitik, whatever such needs might happen to be. But we *do* live in a fragmented world of separate states, and in this world realpolitik is made possible by individual states that "feed" upon the weaknesses of individual persons. There is nothing about the present structure of international relations that makes realpolitik inevitable; it comes about only because this structure combines with behavioral conditions in a way that transforms them both.

In considering this lethal form of synergy, we must not assume that nationalistic feelings are always corrosive, that they always obstruct the requirements of peace and justice. The contributions of nationalism as a force against imperial arrogance and other forms of discrimination and exploitation are well known. It is only when this force oversteps its worthy objectives to become an agent of militarism and interstate conflict that it must be curbed.

It is all a matter of what are customarily described as "stages of development" in world political life. Up to a point, the forces of nationalism represent a progressive influence, serving to supplant oppressive patterns of control with a legitimate expression of national needs and prerogatives. After a time, however, these forces become retrograde, no longer serving vital human needs but rather the contrived "interests" of states, interests that no longer bear any relation to those of individual persons. It is when this happens, when the forces of nationalism become maladaptive, that the requirements of civilization must yield to the more enduring imperatives of planetization.

From the standpoint of modern international law, there is perhaps no more peremptory principle than that of the right to self-determination. Based upon the assumption that this right is the best means to ensure widespread concern for peace and human rights, self-determination is now codified in the Charter of the United Nations as well as in many other instruments adopted by appropriate organs of that body. The UN Charter expressly establishes the right to self-determination in Article 1, paragraph 2 and in Article 55.

Under the Charter, the right to self-determination is seen as an indispensable corrective to the crime of colonialism. Hence, colonial peoples are granted an "inherent" right to struggle by all necessary means, and UN member states are instructed to render all necessary moral and material assistance to the struggle for freedom and independence. In this connection, any action that might interfere with the right of all peoples to the exercise of full sovereignty and to the enjoyment of peace and security is unlawful.

Modern international law also recognizes that the cumulative effect of peoples acting on behalf of their right to self-determination can be international competition and conflict. To temper this effect, it has codified a corollary principle, that of "sovereign equality." Drawn from the eighteenth-century theory of Emerich de Vattel, who reasoned that since people are naturally equal in the condition of nature, so are states, the principle of sovereign equality seeks to ensure respect by each state for every other state. Codified at Article 2, paragraph 1 of the Charter, this principle is the touchstone for a tolerable world order. Since the combined consequences of decentralization and interdependence place great stress on interstate relations, it creates a normative standard that every state should see as self-interested.

Sovereign equality does not mean equality in power and influence, but a *de jure* condition that applies to all states without regard to size, capacity, wealth, economics, or military capability. Moreover, even this condition of sovereign equality is problematic, since the jurisprudential rights of the five permanent members of the Security Council clearly make them "more equal" than all the other states. It follows that although the principle of sovereign equality is for the most part properly conceived, it cannot, by itself, prevent the corrosive transformation of self-determination to militaristic nationalism and xenophobia.

What *can* prevent such transformation are the sorts of steps and remedies already outlined. The path to an improved world order lies promisingly at its human beginnings. With this in mind, it must be understood that the underlying point of contention between the superpowers is not ideological or economic, but a groundless rhetoric reinforced by self-serving elites. Indeed, the rivalry between the United States and the Soviet Union, once spawned and sustained by genuine considerations of purpose and power, is now essentially a contrivance, nurtured by their respective leadership bodies, who may have more in common with each other than with their respective populations. In what is perhaps the greatest single irony of modern world politics, these elites and their defense "community" handmaidens are *true* allies, supporting each other while they undermine the security of both countries. As allies, of course, they do not recognize their mutual support structure and interdependence; there is nothing conspiratorial about their relationship, but it exists nonetheless.

In their mutual relationship, the defense communities of the superpowers coexist in a condition of symbiosis. Each is essential to the health and survival of the other. But in their relationship with their respective societies and with the world as a whole, they are unambiguously parasitic, drawing from that organism which is humanity the very life blood of a species approaching extinction. To ensure that such circumstances remain as they are, the two communities have developed and promoted an arcane nuclear theology, a scriptural system of norms and beliefs upheld by a priesthood of "experts." Since those who exist apart from this priesthood are judged incapable of offering meaningful criticism of the new faith in "nuclearism," their objections are ruled out of order. Planet Earth continues to journey on its rendezvous with omnicide.

But what are the scriptural foundations of this new theology? Above all, they rest on "science," on presumptions of objectivity and rationality that seem unassailable to laypersons. Vitalized by hard data and by the most advanced computer technology, they are promoted by "professionals" who will brook no interference by amateurs, by persons whose solicitude for care and compassion might render them unsuited for the hard and dispassionate calculations needed for survival.

But the "tough-minded" disposition of these professional strategists does not imply genuine understanding. As Hannah Arendt noted some time ago, the new priesthood is cold-blooded enough to consider discomfiting thoughts, but in such consideration it does not really *think*. In Arendt's words:

> Instead of indulging in such an old-fashioned, uncomputerizable activity, they reckon with the consequences of certain hypothetically assumed constellations without, however, being able to test their hypotheses against actual occurrences. The logical flaw in these hypothetical constructions of future events is always the same: what first appears as a hypothesis—with or without its implied alternatives, according to the level of sophistication—turns immediately, usually after a few paragraphs, into a "fact," which then gives birth to a whole string of similar non-facts, with the result that the purely speculative character of the whole enterprise is forgotten. Needless to say, this is not science, but pseudo-science.[8]

Our most profound objection to such pseudo-science, however, is not its limited utility, but its danger, since it presumes an entirely unwarranted degree of understanding and control over events. Since nothing in the world corresponds to the realpolitik advocate's paradigm of state actors who: (1) always choose between alternative courses of action in terms of expected benefits and (2) always use correct information in their decisional calculations, such a paradigm fails to produce its intended effects. An obvious case in point is Vietnam, where an operating presumption of rationality—supported by reports and analyses bristling with technical data, graphs, and tables—led this country to unprecedented disaster.

The conduct of foreign policy according to the realpolitik model necessarily obscures the essential human underpinnings of international behavior. This reminds us of Goethe's wisdom in *Urfaust:*

> All theory, dear friend, is gray,
>
> But the golden tree of life is green.

To understand properly the activities of states, one must keep in mind that they are conducted by thinking, feeling human beings. Although it is true that some measure of dehumanization must be accepted as the cost of theoretical fruitfulness, we must not forget that national leaders sometimes depart from a specified set of rules in reaching decisions or that others may not understand such rules. Since the colorless and ordered universe implied by realpolitik involves the sacrifice of *esprit de finesse,* the ability to perceive human beings in their peculiarly concrete form, it leads not to reason, but to a vast emptiness of dogma. The priesthood that dissolves thought with such dogma has all of the seriousness of any theological elite, but behind its ritualistic incantations there is only blasphemy.

When the sculptor August Rodin began the most ambitious project of his career in 1880, a pair of doors deriving its theme from Dante's allegorical journey through hell, he determined to create a personal vision of the underworld far more complex than that of the *Inferno.* With this vision, hell was to represent a condition rather than a place. Following this conceptual goal, the plaster composition developed to display an agonizing humanity writhing against a changing background. The solitary tranquil form in the work is *The Thinker,* who, from his high position in the lintel, broods on the swarm below as he reviews and reimagines the fate of our species.

As suggested by Rodin, the background of the world, always in flux, is now highlighted by an unprecedented vastness of space, by infinite abysses that mock our insignificance. Viewed from the vantage point of the artist's *Thinker,* this condition compels an end to the egotism of realpolitik imaginings and a beginning to less lethal patterns of consciousness. In these beginnings, the state must be shorn of its trappings of sacredness, and international interactions must be understood solely as more or less transient patterns of mundane limits. In abandoning the ruins of realpolitik ideology, the United States could begin to confront the ashes of endless ruins-in-the-making not as a prospective victim but as a gifted mentor to all who wish to survive.

With its current foreign policy, the United States stands before the world as an impetuous void, a fatality without substance whose plans for success are merely designs for the end of the world. Nothing prepares this country for apocalypse, yet it tends toward it, drawn steadily "forward" by the seductive virulence of a nuclear destiny. Perhaps because until now it has known little more than the sterility of uninterrupted good fortune, America will find it difficult to invest its policy actions with a new kind of lucidity. But there is still time for a change in direction if those who preside over our safety learn to reverse still-advancing superstitions with a less "heroic" vision of international politics. Should the United States proceed to move about in a world that has all of the earmarks of an archaic cosmology, it may continue its exhibitions of effrontery for a time, but they would be no more than a mordant reflex of a profane bravado.

Notes

1. See Thomas S. Kuhn, *The Structure of Scientific Revolutions* (Chicago: The University of Chicago Press, 1962).
2. See Henry Steele Commager, "Machiavelli in the New World," *Worldview* 26, no. 8, August 1983, p. 6.
3. Ibid.
4. See Josiah Strong, *Our Country: Its Possible Future and Its Present Crisis,* pp. 174–175; cited by Richard Hofstadter, *Social Darwinism in American Thought* (Boston: Beacon Press, 1955), p. 179.
5. Cited by Hofstadter, ibid., p. 180.
6. See Erich Fromm, *On Disobedience* (New York: The Seabury Press, 1981), p. 21.
7. See Patrick Riley, ed. and tr., *The Political Writings of Leibniz* (Cambridge, England: Cambridge University Press, 1972), p. 39.
8. See Hannah Arendt, *On Violence* (New York: Harcourt, Brace and World, 1970), p. 7.

Index

About the Author

Louis René Beres, professor of political science at Purdue University, received his Ph.D. at Princeton University in 1971. A specialist in foreign affairs and international law with particular reference to strategic and world order studies, he is the author of many major books and articles in the field. A frequent lecturer in the United States and abroad on matters concerning nuclear weapons, nuclear war, and human rights, he is recognized widely as one of the leading scholars in the worldwide movement for a durable and just peace. His forthcoming books are titled *Principles of World Order Design* and *International Law and the Prevention of Genocide.* Professor Beres was born in Zurich, Switzerland, on August 31, 1945. He now resides in West Lafayette, Indiana, with his wife, Valerie, and daughter Lisa Alexandra.